What Works in Resi
Child Care

A review of research evidence
and the practical considerations

Roger Clough
Roger Bullock
Adrian Ward

national centre for excellence in residential child care

national
children's
bureau

NCB promotes the voices, interests and well-being of all children and young people across every aspect of their lives.

As an umbrella body for the children's sector in England and Northern Ireland, NCB provides essential information on policy, research and best practice for our members and other partners.

NCB aims to:

■ challenge disadvantage in childhood
■ work with children and young people to ensure they are involved in all matters that affect their lives
■ promote multidisciplinary cross-agency partnerships and good practice
■ influence government policy through policy development and advocacy
■ undertake high quality research and work from an evidence-based perspective
■ disseminate information to all those working with children and young people, and to children and young people themselves.

NCB has adopted and works within the UN Convention on the Rights of the Child.

Published by the National Children's Bureau

National Children's Bureau, 8 Wakley Street, London EC1V 7QE
Tel: 020 7843 6000
Website: www.ncb.org.uk
Registered charity number: 258825

© National Children's Bureau 2006

ISBN 1 904787 77 0

British Library Cataloguing in Publication Data
A catalogue record for this book is available from the British Library

The views expressed in this book are those of the authors and not necessarily those of the National Children's Bureau.

Manufactured in the UK by LPPS Ltd, Wellingborough, NN8 3PJ

Contents

Figures

Tables

Foreword and acknowledgements

The review of the evidence from research on practice in the residential care of children and young people was the first stage of a larger review of residential services undertaken for the National Assembly for Wales. The second stage of the work was to consider the implications of the evidence for practice in Wales. This publication, supported by the Welsh Assembly Government, draws together material from the two elements of the project. We make it explicit when our material refers only to Wales.

Linked to the work undertaken on residential child care were studies of foster care. The full reports on both projects can be found on the Children First website of the Welsh Assembly Government:

www.childrenfirst.wales.gov.uk/content/placement/foster-res-care-review-e.pdf

www.childrenfirst.wales.gov.uk/content/placement/foster-res-care-review-stage-2-e.pdf

The work for the Welsh Assembly was overseen by Roger Clough (emeritus professor at Lancaster University and Eskrigge Social Research) and Matthew Colton (professor at Swansea University). Roger Clough led the residential survey and Matthew Colton the fostering. The first chapter of this publication uses material that was part of an introduction to the two reports.

The brief for the residential child care project was to produce:

> a review that considers the purpose and future shape of residential care services for children in Wales with the aim of establishing a cogent theoretical basis and strategic direction for the development of an effective, quality service.

The literature review in this report draws on research that is UK wide, with references to the USA. As we have pointed out, the work was commissioned by the Welsh Assembly Government, and so some parts are presented as a case study. Nevertheless, we think that the key messages are applicable throughout the UK, and leave such extrapolation to the reader.

The project team places on record its thanks to staff from the Welsh Assembly Government for their support to the project and their determination that the project team members should be free to make their own judgements. Of course, the views put forward in this report are the responsibility of the authors of the report and should not be taken to represent the views of the National Assembly for Wales.

We are grateful also to the National Centre for Excellence in Residential Child Care based at the National Children's Bureau for its wish to get this material to a wider audience. The work was undertaken in 2003 and the reports completed early in 2004. We have incorporated some more recent material in this reworking of those reports.

1 Introduction

RESEARCH FOR PRACTICE

There is a proper and vociferous demand that actions taken on behalf of the state to 'look after' children and young people should be based on what is effective in bringing about desired change. Too much of what has taken place, it is argued, has been the consequence of individual beliefs that are not necessarily founded on evidence; further, there has been too little searching to know what is effective.

In this review we aim to set out the state of knowledge of residential care for children and young people, highlighting both what is known and the limits of knowledge. The purpose of the review is to highlight salient features for the development of policy within Wales.

Not surprisingly, the demand for the development of effective practice has led to a search for an 'evidence base' for what is done, and the term 'evidence based' has come into fashion as an indicator of sound practice. Thus, increasingly, it is common for people to claim: 'Research shows … ', followed by a particular viewpoint. We do present the case for the better use of the knowledge that is available. However, we also point out the dangers of many distortions that are made when research findings are muddled or oversimplified.

Research should be designed to advance our understanding of a particular aspect of service provision. But the information that comes from research is not absolute truth. Research may be conducted well or badly; or it may produce probabilities. The value of the findings will be linked to the quality of the research. So in this report we try to pinpoint what is known, together with guidance on the reliability of the information.

ESSENTIAL INFORMATION

The first point, seemingly obvious, is 'How much do we know of the nature of the problem that is presented?' Children (and from here on we shall be using the term 'children' to refer to children and young people) do not begin life needing social services support. At some stage some children will be said 'to need' such assistance. What is known about such needs? How are they defined? It is an obvious fact, but frequently ignored, that planning of services ought to follow categorisation of children's needs. In planning services it is imperative to know the numbers of children with different sorts and patterns of needs so that appropriate services may be developed. This is not to argue that children should be slotted into services. Rather, it is to assert that individual children can only be looked after properly if their needs have been understood and effective services developed in response to them.

Second, given that the needs of children have been defined, are we clear about what it is that intervention on behalf of the state is designed to achieve? What are the hoped for outcomes?

Third, if the desired outcomes are known, is there evidence of how they might best be achieved? We may know, for example, that children benefit from a limited number of moves of substitute placements, but know less about how to achieve that goal.

KNOWLEDGE IN THE CONTEXT OF CHILDREN'S LIVES

Residential provision has to be evaluated in the context of the total lives of children. Too often staff in residential establishments have been castigated for failing to remedy long-standing problems. Of course it is reasonable to ask what can be expected from the period of intervention, taking account of the child's history and home environment. The children who move into residential homes and schools as a consequence of social services intervention are likely to face pervasive problems that have not been easy to manage in other settings. There are numerous examples that illustrate the difficulties.

One situation discussed in several research studies concerns children's education. It is known that many children and families come from a culture that has low educational expectations. It is, therefore, in some ways naïve to imagine that short stays in residential establishments are likely to counter deep-rooted disillusionment and alter views among children, their families and adult carers that education is not particularly important.

Staff in residential homes, even if they succeed in supporting the motivation of the children, cannot ensure the commitment of the children's families or, every bit as important, guarantee that the education authority and local schools will give the children serious attention. Without such support from parts of other systems, the activities of the residential staff are circumscribed. Of course this is not to argue that carers should be complacent about poor educational outcomes for children supposedly looked after by the state. It is perfectly possible to compensate for long-term disadvantage: however, it is essential to recognise the complexity of the task.

A second example is equally powerful. 'Inclusion', properly, is a key term used to capture the idea that people should not *be* excluded, and *see themselves* as denied activities that are central to the lives of their peers. Attempts to understand the experiences of disabled children show clearly that frequently they are excluded by environments, with poor access or inadequate transport limiting their potential to go to certain places. The term 'inclusion' is often used as if it is a single entity whereas in reality it covers different areas of children's lives: poverty, quality of life, need or social relationships. People may be excluded in one area and not in another (Axford 2003).

Two further illustrations reinforce the point that carers, whether foster or residential, cannot on their own ensure a child's inclusion in wider society. While there is now considerable attention paid to respecting children's rights, children in substitute care still face dangers of being excluded in the areas of need, quality of life, poverty and social relationships. Repeatedly they report that they feel that the experience of being looked after by the state demeans them in the eyes of others. Carers may work hard to help children develop their sense of self-worth but they cannot manage the world in which children live.

Morris (2000) notes that young people 'talked about how important it was to influence the attitudes of the general public, because …

all those who work with children are drawn from the ranks of the general public'.

> They should make an advert on TV saying it's nothing big to be in a foster home. Because then people get a better understanding about it. It's like they hear 'There's an alien just landed near London Bridge' – but if you make it known that there's aliens all over the gaff, no-one's going to think it's strange, are they?'
> *(Danny Carter, quoted in Morris 2000, p. 29)*

This marginalisation is exacerbated by the tendency for residential care to be 'excluded' within children's services. The accepted wisdom in the United Kingdom is that fostering is the preferred placement for children unless there are circumstances that militate against it. Whether or not this results in children and staff from residential establishments feeling more excluded than their counterparts in foster homes remains uncertain.

In any review of research evidence, therefore, there is a further critical point to be made about knowledge in context: findings are not absolute truths but are products of their time, conditioned by knowledge in other areas.

Tizard (1986) provides a powerful example of such changed understanding. She re-examined the influential work of Bowlby, pointing out both its limitations and its continuing relevance. Bowlby had argued that young children faced significant problems if they were deprived of attachment to their mothers at critical periods in infancy. Tizard reviewed later research, which demonstrated that Bowlby had underplayed the role of fathers and underplayed the potential for attachment to others than the mother. Nevertheless, Tizard recognised the vital relevance of 'attachment' as a concept to explain aspects of development. She considered three ways in which staff in day nurseries could provide better care for children: familiarity (getting to know children, including their likes and habits), responsiveness and attachment. The relevance of such ideas to the quality of relationship between carers and children in residential homes will be considered later.

A further danger to the certainties that may be ascribed to research occurs as researchers move from analysis to recommendation. Parker's (1966) early work on fostering showed that there were more fostering breakdowns when children of the foster carers were of similar age to the foster child. This has been cited as grounds for not placing foster children in families where there are similar-aged children. It is not clear from subsequent studies how significant this risk is, but it needs to be considered. An alternative response, therefore, is to recognise the potential difficulties in such placements and ensure that special attention is given to dealing with them.

OUTCOMES AND EVIDENCE

Managers and practitioners in children's services want to know 'What works for children?' Using this phrase as the title for one review of research, McNeish, Newman and Roberts (2002) offer a definition of evidence-based child care practice that should form the basis of such knowledge:

> the process of systematically locating, critically reviewing and using research findings as the basis for decisions in child care practice. (p. 3)

Basing decisions on evidence is, therefore, an essential part of good practice. However, as noted earlier, we have to be alert to considerations of the quality of the evidence and the fact that findings may not be as authoritative or unequivocal as they first appear. In medicine the traditional means of collecting evidence as to the efficacy of treatments is through randomised controlled trials in which a population with similar characteristics is divided into two groups: one is given the treatment to be tested; the other has no treatment at all or a placebo (a supposed treatment which in reality has no known effect). Trials of this type are rarely, if ever, conducted in social care but without them, it is difficult to prove effects. Without more studies of this type, researchers will find it difficult to tell practitioners what they want to know: that is, what works? (Little, Kohm and Thompson 2005). As one of us has written:

> There are major debates in the research literature as to the nature of truth: are some methods of collecting data more reliable than others? At its most simple, one group has been described as *positivists*, in that they seek for information which has scientific validity: given x and y, z will always follow. Others argue that people's experiences are not like that and to search for a presumed scientific objectivity distorts what happens. To understand people, they would contend, you must take account of their perceptions of what has happened (and what it means to them). …

> Research is not truth: it aims to describe and explain, but remains an interpretation of material by the researcher. Researchers differ not only in methods but also in their skills. Some are better able than others to get people to talk about their work or to see significant clues through their observation.
> *(Clough 2000, p. 137)*

It is also important for people interpreting research to be aware of the different ways in which information is collected: some may be in the form of statistics (for example, the numbers of moves for a child) and others in a form that describes experiences (for example, the views of children and carers on the reasons for or impacts of moves). There are varying types of evidence, ranging from single case studies of a particular place, via accounts of personal experiences from staff and adults who, as children, had lived in residential homes, to larger, comparative cohort studies.

Even when evidence has been gathered, there are difficulties in interpreting evidence about the effects of interventions. For example, there may be observable benefits but these may not be the result of the intervention itself. More important may be what goes with it, such as the interest by other people or the enjoyment of the experience. This so-called Hawthorne effect is what produces the change, not the intervention. So some critics of residential care would say that if you want to make children happy, there is no need to put them through the rigours of treatment; giving them money or taking them on a holiday will achieve the same results. This is why many politicians and professionals outside social work are suspicious of measures of consumer satisfaction being used as a criterion for 'success'.

An additional problem is that many behavioural and emotional disorders have periods of remission. A psychologically troubled young person often settles in a placement for a while before difficulties recur. Follow-up studies might just hit on a remission period and so find atypically good results. The teenage mother delighted with her new baby may be more fraught when her offspring becomes a grizzly toddler. Differences in the time period for a follow-up study of treatments can produce quite different results.

A further complication is whether we can be certain that we are comparing 'like with like' cases. If high and low risk groups are mixed, the composition of the sample will affect the outcomes. In children's services in the United Kingdom, the increasing use of adoption for highly vulnerable young children, combined with family support for those able to leave care quickly, means that those who remain in care for long periods, which includes most young people in residential establishments, are more likely to have complex and enduring needs. Thus when considering studies of children in different types of residential care or experiencing other interventions, we need to be sure that children with the same needs, at the same level of severity, are being compared. Otherwise we might attribute any findings to the care setting rather than to the background of the children.

In summary, we accept the argument that practice based on demonstrable effectiveness is both desirable and a right for children and their families. However, we remain conscious of the difficulties of measurement, analysis and interpretation.

2 Residential child care research: the state of knowledge

TRENDS IN RESEARCH INTO RESIDENTIAL CHILD CARE

It is useful initially to outline some broad trends in research of residential homes to show the search for different sorts of understanding. Following the publication of Goffman's 1961 book *Asylums*, people looked for the ways in which all residential homes had common characteristics, for example a tendency to strip 'inmates' of their own identity and assert that of the establishment, to separate staff and children into 'them' and 'us', and to look after people in groups rather than individually. Thus people wanted to know what it was about residential establishments (termed 'institutions' in what has become a pejorative term) that resulted in certain practices that militated against individualised care. What was forgotten as people looked for common characteristics was that there were also many factors which made places different from one another.

Previous reviews of research

The literature on residential child care divides somewhat uncomfortably between the research and the theory. We will discuss these elements separately before exploring the potential overlap.

Two previous reviews of the literature on residential child care are worth noting. The first (Bullock, Little and Millham 1993) divides the research literature into two main periods: from 1960 to 1975, and from 1975 to 1992. The first of these periods, culminating in the publication of

Varieties of Residential Experience (Tizard, Sinclair and Clarke 1975), was characterised by a number of studies of regimes, examining their 'ethos' and culture, and their impacts on staff and residents, though not usually in terms of post-care outcomes. Among the themes noted is that, within the residential settings, the 'informal cultures created by staff and children are especially significant in influencing performance' (Bullock, Little and Millham 1993, p. 8). During the period from 1975–92, the authors argue that the focus of research moved away from *regimes* and towards the *functions* of residential care for the wider child care system. There was some interest in the longer-term effects and outcomes of care, although the difficulties inherent in studying the multiple factors influencing outcomes were well recognised.

The second research review, *Caring for Children Away From Home* (Department of Health 1998) covers 12 separate but linked studies commissioned by the Department of Health (DH) and others during the period 1995 to 1998. This study, subtitled *Messages from Research*, provides a systematic overview of these projects and of their implications for the planning of services, although it emphasises that uniform edicts or 'sweeping pronouncements about the organisation of residence or the theoretical approach are of limited value' (p. 26). The main messages are about the importance of well-articulated objectives that are consistent throughout the organisation, clear and coherent leadership and appropriate contact with family members. This review also includes a set of 24 recommendations for improving practice, together with a number of exercises for managers and practitioners getting them to explore 'Are the findings true for us?' The implicit argument is that in many respects before we can even address the question 'What works in residential care?', we need to be much clearer as to 'What *happens*?'

The DH overview notes the context in which residential homes exist, in particular that several of the boundaries between residence and fostering had become blurred, for example in terms of size, expertise, length of stay and payment. Indeed, the authors suggest that the term 'children's home' is no longer useful because places called 'children's homes' are so different. They suggest that 'residence' is a preferable description. The one distinguishing feature between residence and fostering remains that foster carers provide facilities in their own homes.

The authors try 'to identify the conditions in which residence can be shown to be beneficial' (p. 5). They continue:

> This book is not ... a comforting read. It describes much that is wrong
> with residence, mitigated to a degree by some strong indications of how
> it can be improved. (p. 6)

A third review is that of Berridge (2002) who looked at the evidence of
'what works' for children in residential care. This review consists largely
of an overview of the two major reviews discussed above, although it
does draw some useful further conclusions, especially in terms of the
question of leadership. Berridge emphasises the research findings that
the role of the head of a home is very influential in determining the
quality of care, not only in terms of the formal role but also in terms of
their personal and professional qualities. He also identifies the lack of
specialist or therapeutic input for many children in residential homes,
despite evidence of great need.

Bullock and colleagues argued in 1993 that 'gaps left by recent
research cannot be filled by knowledge gained from the pre-1975
studies, because residential establishments have changed so much
since the 1960s' (1993, p. 11), and the same might be said about the
period from 1993 to 2003: residential services have declined further in
use, and changed further in terms of size, age range and purpose of
unit. Nevertheless, some of the key principles underlying the provision
of the best residential care probably remain the same throughout and
were well summarised in the Social Services Inspectorate (SSI)
report in 1993 on the national selective inspections of children's
homes:

> the effectiveness of staff in those homes where good practice was
> observed was based on clear leadership, organised and consistent ways
> of working, and clarity of purpose.
> *(SSI 1993, p. 31)*

Research into the mental health needs of children and young people

The reviews discussed covered primarily the social and structural
dimensions of residential child care. Other reviews have addressed
specific aspects of children's needs, especially their education and
physical and mental health. The last of these is perhaps especially
significant for the present discussion. In particular, Meltzer and
others (2002), in *The Mental Health of Young People Looked After*

by Local Authorities in England, examine the literature as well as conducting an authoritative survey of the field. Among the studies discussed is one by McCann and others (1996) who reported that 57 per cent of Oxfordshire children in foster care and 96 per cent of adolescents in residential care (median time in care 2 years 10 months) showed some form of psychiatric disorder, a significant number of which had gone undetected; included in these figures were 23 per cent of those in residential care assessed as having a major depressive disorder. A study by Dimigen and others (1999) of 5–12 year olds entering foster or residential care in Glasgow, found 'very elevated levels of conduct, depression and other disorders', with many of the children having more than one disorder. The authors comment that 'a considerable proportion of young children have a serious psychiatric disorder at the time they enter local authority care but are not being referred for psychological help' (p. 675). Among young people in residential care, Meltzer and others report figures of 17.7 per cent, 56.2 per cent and 7.2 per cent for emotional disorders, conduct disorder and hyperkinetic disorders respectively.

Research into the experiences of children and staff

A final tranche of research looks at residential care from the point of view of staff and children. These take many forms. For example, Baldwin (1990) explored with staff why they could not practise what they knew to be right, and care leavers have described their experiences in many different ways, including novels, television documentaries and contributions to qualitative research studies. Methodologies have moved on since the classic texts of *The Hothouse Society, Growing Up in Care* and *Who Cares?* (Lambert and Millham 1968; Kahan 1979 and Page 1978) and the child's view is now almost a sine qua non of any child care project, although interestingly recent changes in education have mostly sought to strengthen the influence of parents' rather than children's views.

Much of the discussion in these accounts focuses on relationships, whether between children and staff or among peers. Berridge has emphasised the importance of these for 'what works'. He notes that in the field of foster care people 'talk of the chemistry between carers and individual children, which can make for a successful placement, sometimes against the odds.' He continues:

recent research has sought to explain this using attachment theory. ...
Several of the studies of residential homes explained successful
residential care according to the quality of the interaction between young
people and adults. Terms used include: empathy; approachability;
persistence; willingness to listen and reliability.
(Berridge 2002, p. 100)

McNeish, Newman and Roberts (2002, p. 276) also write of the
attributes of positive and enduring relationships:

> the ability of a worker to have a laugh, to communicate informally and to
> demonstrate commitment to the young person. An essential ingredient ...
> was the young person feeling as if the adult genuinely cared – that they
> were there for them and not just doing their job.

Similarly, a young person describes how important and empowered he
felt when his views were taken seriously in a review (Morris 2000, p. 31).

A novel attempt to combine the child's view with statistical research
evidence is found in *A Life Without Problems: The achievements of a
therapeutic community* (Little and Kelly 1995), in which the findings are
informed by a juxtaposition of quantitative evidence on children's care
careers and a teenage girl's diary.

THE STRENGTHS AND LIMITATIONS OF RESEARCH KNOWLEDGE

The previous discussions suggest that there is an authoritative body of
research regarding many aspects of residential care but that fashions
result in there being more information on some types of setting than
others. In the 1960s the focus was on approved (reform) schools and
secure units. This shifted to children's homes in the 1980s and 1990s.
But there has been comparatively little research on special schools,
now taking larger numbers of children than community homes.

While this available knowledge is welcome, it has to be acknowledged
that even in areas where researchers are relatively confident, much of
the dominant view of the value of residential care for children is shaped
by other sources of information, especially the focus on well-publicised
failures and the consequent enquiries.

But, even in areas where researchers are confident, two other aspects are critical in understanding research into looked after children. The first is that while there is significant evidence of factors that contribute to successful outcomes, there is less research into how to deliver them. We know, as will be reported later, that the quality of relationship between carer and child is critical to success, but are less sure of how to produce a good-quality relationship: what combination of carer characteristics, organisational aspects and child response produces 'the good relationship'? Do we know enough to be able to select appropriate people as carers or, organisationally, to know how to support them?

Second, it is important in research to distinguish the delineation of outcome results from theoretical explanations of them. Brown and colleagues (1998) studied nine homes and developed indicators of performance which include:

■ the ways staff, children and others see the home
■ the ways staff and children are seen to behave in the home
■ the quality of practice in relation to standards specified by the Children Act 1989.

They found that the homes that did best on nearly all the criteria were:

> those with concordant societal, formal and belief goals, strong positive staff cultures and either strong positive child cultures or ones that were fragmented without undermining the work of the establishment. (p. 138)

Thus, one outcome result from that research is that concordant beliefs and strong positive staff cultures produce a positive impact on performance. This finding appears to apply generally, whatever the particular belief systems or theoretical explanations of children's problems that underpin the work of the establishment. Obviously, outcomes for children further improve if these conditions underpin a regime known to be effective at meeting their particular needs. This finding matches well with the sorts of observations that many of us would make when visiting establishments: those places that we rate highly have positive staff and child cultures, and have clear theories as to the reasons why children behave as they do and what are the best treatment approaches. However, their theoretical bases are likely to differ one from another.

The foregoing sections suggest that residential child care is a field which has been adequately researched but inadequately theorised. To be more precise, we now have a reasonable baseline of information about the structure and nature of existing services, about whom they are for and what happens in them, but we still know little about the details of the processes involved, their outcomes or about how these outcomes may be best achieved. So while we have a certain amount of knowledge, we are still relatively short of ideas as to what will help to improve services, especially ideas that have been tested in practice.

Walton and Elliott's collection *Residential Care: A reader in current theory and practice* (1980) was widely used in the past by residential staff. In it individual writers described practice and theorised about their work. Comparatively little work has followed this approach. There are some theories *for* practice (guidance for staff and students as to how certain types of situation should be handled or planned for) and theories *about* practice (analysing the task, its components, its context and its implications), but there is not much that analyses or theorises as to how different types of home should be structured and managed, or how the fine detail of care should be delivered. Immediate examples come to mind: how should respite care be delivered, or what sort of residential organisation will best enable children to be 'prepared' for family placement? Brown and others probably come closest to this perspective when they describe the connections between 'structures and cultures', but their work is necessarily limited by the relatively small number and range of homes studied.

DIFFICULTIES IN COMPARING ESTABLISHMENTS AND SYSTEMS

It is important to note that it is difficult to make comparisons between homes and care systems even within the United Kingdom, let alone internationally. Such comparisons are made at times but the terminology used to describe both the characteristics of children and the systems or style of homes and schools is not standardised, and this makes valid comparisons problematic. There have been frequent attempts to distinguish one group of children from another. Sometimes this is by age, which, along with sex, is perhaps the only factor that can be seen as unproblematic. The distinctions matter because systems and treatments may be based on them. Looking at the development of services for children since the early 19th century we see children separated from adults with the development of reformatory schools to save them from the contamination of prison; girls separated from boys; and separate provision (industrial schools) to take those in need of 'care and protection' as opposed to those who had committed offences and went to reformatory schools. This has some similarities with later descriptions of children as 'troubled' or 'troublesome' (Whittaker 1979).

Similarly, some distinctions that have attempted to define the causation of the child's behaviour have led to children receiving contrasting placements. Thus in the past some children have been termed 'maladjusted', a label that was likely to lead to different treatment from being labelled 'delinquent'. The former went to a maladjusted school under the auspices of the education system, the latter to approved schools or community homes run successively by children's and social services departments or under the auspices of the Home Office. In part definition and career have been influenced by the routes that families and professionals wanted the child to take.

However, it has also been increasingly recognised that children do not fit neatly into such categories; they may be both troubled and troublesome. In addition, we have to recognise that apart from administrative categories created by legislation there has been no agreement as to what terms mean: different people have different interpretations of characteristics. Thus, even within the United Kingdom it is very difficult to be sure that a child described in certain terms by one professional is similar to a child described in the same language by another. Without a common language to understand children's needs, a term such as 'vulnerable' can conjure up risks as varied as predisposition to genetically inherited illness, dangers of abuse and neglect or likelihood of offending or drug abuse, depending on the professional using the term. Inevitably, the problem is compounded when attempting to make international comparisons.

A common example of such confusion is found when considering US programmes for young offenders in residential care. There are several studies of 'New Careers' projects (by which offenders obtain training and jobs) and of policies that seek to deter teenagers from crime by showing them adult prisons. In both cases success has been claimed in US research studies, and interest has been shown in copying them in the United Kingdom. But evidence on young people's backgrounds suggests that in the USA there are more socialised delinquents (that is, deprived youths influenced by poverty and peer pressure) in such programmes than in the United Kingdom, where those in residential care or custody are more likely to have more severe psychological and social problems. Thus, the young people in the US samples are better candidates for approaches that simply widen opportunities or deter by fear.

Another illustration, a careful comparison between fostering and residential care, shows how terminology can mask similarities between systems. In the 1940s and 1950s a system frequently adopted for the running of a children's home was for there to be two houseparents living in the establishment, typically with the wife being at home and the husband going out to work. The children would share the lives of the houseparents: work and living for the houseparents were intertwined. In the 1960s increasingly this pattern was criticised on the grounds that staff became too involved with the children; it was thought important to separate personal and professional lives. Staff were first encouraged and then required to set up their own home off the premises of the children's home and come in to work each day.

But alongside this development was a wish to maintain children in 'ordinary' circumstances when possible: and so for most, fostering was to be preferred to children's homes. The irony is that today many children's homes are running with very small numbers of children (in some cases as few as one or two children) while foster homes take ever larger groups, some with five to seven children. The foster carers live in their own home and share their lives with the children: thus reinventing the personal and professional intermix that caused concern previously.

DISAGGREGATING RESIDENTIAL CARE FOR CHILDREN

Several attempts have been made to disaggregate residential provision for children so that the aims, structures and effects of particular types of establishments can be better understood. The value of any classification is to explain empirical reality and facilitate exploration of the effects of residence on staff, children and families. Thus, no classification is correct in its own right, it depends on whether it explains or informs the questions asked. Managers might want to know how many beds are needed or how far regimes meet national standards, practitioners might seek good outcomes, while the public might be concerned with child protection or control.

EXPLORING THE VARIETY OF PROVISION

Initially, it is clear that there is considerable variety in the types of residential provision used for children. It is difficult to define precisely what constitutes residence as some children board weekly and spend school holidays at home. However, the 1996 survey by Gooch showed that 128,000 children aged 0–18 begin each day in England and Wales with an institutional breakfast. This shows a 45 per cent fall since Moss's earlier 1971 survey (Tizard, Sinclair and Clarke 1975).

However, this fall has not been consistent across sectors. The reduction has been greatest in children's homes, provision for children and independent boarding schools but less for children in special education, hospitals and youth custody.

The 1996 figures for children aged 0–18 in residential establishments in England and Wales are shown in Table 2.1.

Table 2.1 Children in residential establishments, 1996

Context	Number (thousands)
Children's homes	7
Boarding special schools	21
Provision for disabled children	2
Young offender institutions	2
Boarding schools (not special)	84
Hospitals	12
TOTAL	128

Source: Gooch (1996).

Table 2.2 shows more recent figures for the location of looked after children in England 2002.

Table 2.2 Children looked after on 31 March 2002, England

	ALL	Age 0–10	Age 10–15	Age 16–18	All aged 10–18
Units/homes/ hostels	6,800 (11.4%)	400 (1.6%)	4,200 (16.6%)	2,200 (23.2%)	6,400 (18.4%)
Other centres	650 (1.1%)	150 (0.6%)	230 (0.9%)	260 (2.7%)	490 (1.4%)
Schools	1,100 (1.8%)	80 (0.3%)	760 (3.0%)	280 (2.9%)	1,040 (3.0%)
TOTAL	8,550	630	5,190	2,740	7,930
Total looked after	59,700	24,800	25,300	9,500	34,800
% in residential care	14.3%	2.5%	20.5%	28.8%	22.8%

Source: DH statistics on children looked after by local authorities.

It can be seen from the Table 2.2 that in 2002, overall, 14 per cent of all the looked after children were living in a residential home. However, very low numbers of children under 10 years of age (2.5 per cent) were in such establishments, whereas nearly 23 per cent of those aged over 10 were living residentially. It is particularly noticeable that nearly 30 per cent of looked after young people aged over 15 were in residential placements. If the 3,000 15–18 year olds in prison are also added in, there is evidence of a more sizeable group of 16–18 year olds in residence of some kind than is usually recognised.

In Wales there were 123 local authority children's homes in 1980, but only 43 in 2001. The fall in numbers of available places in the same period was from 1,664 to 203, while the fall in the numbers of residents on 31 March of the respective years was from 1,445 to 211. Of course these figures list the numbers only in local authority homes (SSDA 903). (See Table 2.3.)

When the ages of looked after children over the period 1980–2001 are compared (Table 2.4), it is found that there has been an increase in the proportion of younger children in care and accommodation, a change that has been accompanied by a fall from 67 to 59 per 100,000 in the rate of children in the wider population who are looked after.

Table 2.3 Children looked after by local authorities by placement, 31 March in respective years, Wales

	Foster placement	Community homes	Private or voluntary homes	With parents or family	Placed for adoption	Retained, detained	Independent accommo- dation	Other	Total
1980	1,709	1,445	153	1,207			88	259	4,861
1992	2,038	468	20	380	82		96	77	3,161
1997	2,303	232	5	289	93		106	262	3,290
2001*	2,690	211	24	408	176	73**	52	83	3,644

* Excluding children in agreed short term placements.

** Not included in total.

Source: SSDA 903.

Table 2.4 Children looked after by local authorities, 31 March 2001, by age groups, Wales

	Under 1	1–4	5–9	10–15	16–17	18 and over	Total
1980	2%	9%	18%	45%	25%	1%	4,861
2001	3%	18%	26%	40%	12%	1%	3,931

In 2003 the numbers of children's homes by sector were as shown in Table 2.5.

Table 2.5 Number of children's homes and places by sector, Wales

Sector	Number of children's homes	Number of places
Private	66	112
Voluntary	10	24
Local authority	43	211
Boarding	8	216
TOTAL	127	563

The total amount of time spent by Welsh children in residential homes and the costs of such stays is also of interest: in the year 2001–2 children had 16,028 weeks' accommodation in homes at a cost of just under £34 million.

YOUTH JUSTICE PROVISION

Three types of secure provision are currently used for the placements of young people: secure training centres (STCs), young offender institutions (YOIs), and local authority secure children's homes (LASCHs). The statements of their functions are as follows.

Secure training centres

STCs are purpose-built centres for young offenders up to the age of 17. They are run by private operators according to Home Office contracts, which set out detailed operational requirements. Currently, there are three STCs in England.

They house vulnerable young people who are sentenced to custody in a secure environment where they can be educated and rehabilitated. They differ from young offender institutions (YOIs) in that they have a higher staff to young offender ratio (minimum of three staff members to eight trainees) and are smaller in size, which means that individuals' needs can be met more easily. The regimes in STCs are constructive and education-focused. They provide tailored programmes for young offenders that give them the opportunity to develop as individuals which, in turn, will help stop them re-offending.

All services related to the operation of an STC are provided on-site, including all education and training, primary healthcare, dentistry, and services to address the young person's offending behaviour (including input from mental health and social care professionals). To facilitate the young person's rehabilitation into the community, STCs have a dedicated team of people working on fostering links with the young person's home community; this is particularly useful in creating educational and employment opportunities on release.

Young offender institutions

YOIs are facilities run by the prison service. They accommodate 15–21 year olds. The Youth Justice Board is only responsible for placing young people under 18 years of age in secure accommodation. Consequently, some of these institutions accommodate older young people than STCs and LASCHs. YOIs have lower ratios of staff to young people than STCs and LASCHs, and generally accommodate larger numbers of young people. Consequently, they are less able to address the individual needs of young people. YOIs are generally considered to be inappropriate accommodation for more vulnerable young offenders.

Local authority secure children's homes

LASCHs focus on attending to the physical, emotional and behavioural needs of young people sent to them. They provide young people with support tailored to their individual needs. To achieve this, they have a high ratio of staff to young people, and are generally small facilities – ranging from five to 38 beds. LASCHs are generally used to accommodate young offenders aged 12–14, girls up to the age of 16, and 15–16 year old boys who are assessed as vulnerable.

There have been several evaluations of secure facilities for young people, such as that by Hagell, Hazel and Shaw (2000) who studied and followed up leavers from the Medway Secure Training Centre. They found mixed results which echo many other studies, such as Little's (1990) *Young Men in Prison* and Bullock and colleagues' (1998) scrutiny of leavers from youth treatment centres.

On the positive side, difficult teenagers were contained in safe and secure conditions, the standard of care was generally high, trainees were generally satisfied with the provision and the education provision improved as time went on. However, on the negative side, some professionals thought that the offending behaviour programme was insufficiently challenging, preparations for release were inadequate, liaison with local youth offending teams and work with families proved difficult, and there were inadequate planning and poor communication between the agencies responsible for supervising the detention and training sentence. The outcomes for behavioural change were also poor, although probably no worse than for other interventions with similar young people, especially as Little and colleagues (2004) have shown in a randomised controlled trial that while alternatives to custody are constructive and cheaper, they cannot be expected to reduce custody on their own.

In a review of the secure estate, Pitts (2005) has also stressed the damage, distress and debilitation of custody in terms of drug use, mental health, violent victimisation, educational and vocational attainment, and deterioration in young offenders' family relationships. He expressed concern about the results of secure services since all these factors are known to be associated with abstention from, or persistence in, crime.

RESIDENTIAL HOMES FOR DISABLED CHILDREN

Discussions about residential provision for children with disabilities are confounded by the varied use of the term 'disability'. If a wide view is taken in which disability includes behavioural and emotional disorders, it is well established that disabled children are over-represented in residential care, remain in residential placements longer than their non-disabled peers, and account for a significant proportion of local authority spending on residential care. Anecdotal evidence suggests that increasing numbers of children with disabilities are moving into residential homes and doing so at a much younger age. Within Wales it is recognised that there is not an accurate picture of either the numbers of children with disabilities in residential care or their characteristics (Social Services Inspectorate for Wales (SSIW) 2003). The same is likely to be true for other countries in the United Kingdom.

In the Welsh report (SSIW 2003), topics that are familiar in general discussion of residential child care are repeated in this sector, with placements being driven by vacancies, crisis responses (even though the children were well known to authorities) and lack of strategic planning:

> The assessment of need is constantly being over ridden by service considerations such as available vacancies in residential units, lack of foster carers and ease of funding mechanisms. There is limited consideration of the needs and views of the child.

> It appeared that emergency and crisis placements were common for disabled children even though they had been known for several years. One participant talked about a situation where personal information relating to the child's needs did not arrive until after the placement had been in place for some time. This did not seem to be an isolated incident.

> Several participants felt that there was a complete lack of strategic planning based on identified trends in relation to services for disabled children and that corporate parenting responsibilities were not fulfilled. *(SSIW 2003)*

For disabled children, some recognised general problems are compounded by a failure to plan for special needs. Inadequate equipment in a family's own home might lead to an otherwise unnecessary residential placement, as might the problems when children move between separated parents and equipment is only provided in one household.

Short breaks in residential care are used for two reasons. Traditionally the main focus has been to provide a break for family carers, and most research has been focused on the extent to which such breaks are valued by those carers. In foster care, apart from the problems of provision, such as failure to plan ahead and insufficient provision, nearly all carers report positively on such schemes (Statham and Greenfields 2005).

There has, in contrast, been comparatively little attention given to whether breaks benefit the children themselves. Increasingly, there is emphasis on the positive aspects of such breaks, providing 'a continuum of opportunities' for disabled children:

> to have new experiences, make new friends and enjoy their free time. Included are pre and after school play, childminding, sitting, individual and group leisure activities, holidays and play schemes and overnight stays (respite care) away from home. Breaks are provided by volunteers, sitters, sessional workers, home care workers, residential care staff, nursing staff and foster carers. Short Breaks are part of a family support strategy that spans a wider range of services designed to meet the needs of all family members.
> *(SSIW 2003)*

The use of residential educational placements for children with disabilities, as for other looked after children, is reported to be influenced by the availability of local services as well as the family's and child's needs. It is not surprising that children with complex health needs, those with what is described as 'challenging behaviour' and those from ethnic minorities wait longest for a service. Further dilemmas that are highlighted again have parallels with other services for children and adults:

- a focus on providing more intensive services for fewer people leaves numbers of people without core, basic services
- the impact of legislation is complex in terms of understanding and impact
- systems are complex, and it may be difficult to access services
- health and safety requirements may interfere with normal, daily living practices
- there are debates as to where responsibility rests between different departments, in particular between health and social services
- there are grand statements about inclusion, but these are difficult to achieve.

There is also uncertainty about when specialist, and separate, provision is in the best interests of a child.

TRENDS IN RESIDENTIAL CHILD CARE

With regard to the changes in usage of residential homes and of the classification systems, at least a dozen separate trends within the residential sector as a whole can be identified (Gooch 1996). In the list that follows we draw on Gooch's findings, but amend them to take account of more recent trends:

- the replacement of single-sex establishments by ones that were co-educational but which, in practice, were dominated by boys; most now include gender as one of the selection criteria in their statement of purpose, and mixed establishments would once again now be in a minority
- the increasing age of residents at entry, though recently there has been a small increase in places focusing on younger children
- an increase in young people with health problems, behaviour disorders and disabilities
- greater racial and ethnic mix
- larger catchment areas, raising problems for educational continuity and contact with home
- more provision by private agencies
- less specialisation by sector, with a resulting mix of needs in each establishment; more recently a growth of establishments focusing on what is defined as a problem area in behaviour terms (challenging behaviour, victims of, or perpetrators of abuse) or on a diagnosed problem (autistic spectrum disorders)
- assessment by need criteria rather than social role categories, such as disability or special educational needs
- a more generalist service
- shorter stays
- rising costs
- more concerns about rights and protection
- further reductions in the size of units and in the numbers accommodated by the system, but a larger proportion of the total places in secure accommodation or other specialist centres such as therapeutic communities.

Naturally, the factors that explain changes in the use of private boarding schools, establishments for children with special educational needs or penal institutions may be different from those that affect child care establishments but in all of these sectors viable alternatives have been created. Even in those primarily concerned with delinquent and disruptive adolescents, the emergence of a coherent youth offending service has been important, although this still relies on residence as a last resort.

CLASSIFICATION OF RESIDENTIAL HOMES

Several attempts have been made to classify residential establishments for children. These exercises have had three main aims:

- to understand better the variety in residential provision, for example differences in size, lengths of stay or aims
- to sharpen definitions of types of establishment so that the relationship between provision and children's needs, services offered and outcomes can be explored more effectively
- to clarify what determines organisational structures; the aim is to achieve greater congruence between the components of the structure and a closer match between aims and methods.

Classifications have used several criteria. These include:

- *administrative category*: for example, health, education, social services, youth custody
- *aims or goals*: for example, whether confined to specific therapy or tasks or concerned with wider aspects of young people's lives
- *functions for young people and for the wider child welfare service*: for example, respite, assessment, shelter, permanence, protection, custody or preparation for further work
- *regimes*: how aims and functions are put into operation.

Several other more specific criteria have also been used. They include size, staff numbers and training, length of stay, nature of entry (for example, coercive or voluntary) and institutional totality.

Specific examples of classifications are provided by several researchers. In 1975, Tizard and colleagues explored ways of better linking organisational factors with effects. They argued that single case studies and 'steam press' models (which looked for similarities between places and ended up forcing establishments into moulds) made it difficult to explain what was producing what. They acknowledged the difficulty posed by the fact that 'variations among residential institutions are such as to defy analysis, and the best we can do is to interpret rather than explain their diversity'. But they insist that common sense is not enough. For example, they say that it did not clarify which of the two then-prevailing models of helping autistic children was best.

They identify four dimensions on which residential establishments differ:

- *ideological:* the prevailing values and beliefs as implemented by staff and managers
- *organisational:* the way aims and values are enshrined in structures and staff roles
- *staffing:* the characteristics, training and attitudes of staff
- *residents' responses:* for example, whether there is learning or socialisation.

These differences are manifest in the characteristics of different establishments. For example:

- establishments with different ideologies tend to recruit and train their own staff, and promote shared values
- organisations differ in the autonomy they grant to staff to make decisions and this affects the prescription and performance of roles
- staffing is a variable in terms of not just background and qualification but also personality and skill
- residents' responses are important because they affect behaviour and role performance.

It can be seen that these four dimensions are inter-related so that certain aspects go together. For example, an ideology of substitute family care is likely to attract staff with certain beliefs, be organised in certain ways and encourage certain responses from the children. An ideology of custody or temporary shelter would produce a different pattern.

At the same time as Tizard was producing this categorisation, Lambert and colleagues (1975) tried to classify boarding schools, ranging from independent public schools to establishments educating children with social needs, but not special schools.

They first considered the aims or goals of the establishment, arguing that it is helpful to define three types of goal: *instrumental* (concerned with the development of skills, such as literacy or qualifications), *expressive* (concerned with end states such as social responsibility for pastoral care) and *organisational* (the aims necessary to keep the establishment viable, such as discipline or administration). It was the balance between these three types of goal that differentiated the schools. Public schools put an emphasis on all three goals; self-styled progressive schools emphasised the expressive at the expense of others; vocational schools devoted resources to instrumental areas; and a few schools seemed obsessed with their own organisational structure and survival.

The factors influencing the pattern of goals pursued were the functions of the establishment. In Lambert's boarding schools these were *allocative* (allocation to social class or educational advancement), *integrative* (socialisation to values) and *administrative* (meeting a welfare need). These functions were enshrined in staff roles and styles of communication, the controls employed, the delegation of authority to residents, subdivision of structure, relationships between the formal culture and the inner world of children and staff, and the ability of the establishment to change. A value of this approach is that knowledge about one area enables prediction about others. Hence, expressive organisations will value expressive staff roles, such as care staff or chaplains, and devote resources to these areas; highly organisational establishments such as remand centres will be quite different in all aspects.

An elaborate classification of the functions of child care establishments was also made by Beedell in 1970. He identified at least 11 distinct functions that represent a mixture of those proposed by Lambert, Tizard and others. They are physical care, safety, control, education, relationships, stability, relief to the wider child care system, shelter, containment, assessment and group work.

A fourth categorisation is provided by Berridge (1985), who found that the main functions of the 20 children's homes he studied in the early 1980s were aiding reception to care, controlling difficult adolescents, caring for groups of siblings, rehabilitating long-stay children and dealing with the aftermath of placement breakdowns.

The most rigorous classification of British and North American establishments for children was undertaken by researchers at the Chapin Hall Center for Children in the University of Chicago (Chipenda-Dansokho and others 2003). In a review of extensive empirical evidence, they produced three dimensions which, independent of one another, appeared to differentiate residential provision most effectively. (Many other dimensions were significant but they tended to be closely related to the three identified.)

They conclude that residential provision can best be divided according to:

■ *The needs of the children being met* – for example, educational, health, behaviour, relationships, protection.
■ *The organisational structure used to make the provision* – for example, the size, kinds of staff employed and way in which provision of care is sub-divided.
■ *The extent and nature of parental involvement and autonomy.*

A statistical cluster analysis of variables associated with these three dimensions was then undertaken.

Initially, it became clear that establishments with a single aim and function, such as a short-stay hospital or remand centre, were difficult to classify in the same framework used for other establishments, and were best dealt with as a separate category. For establishments with more than one function, a five-fold typology emerged:

1. Facilities that are primarily focused on providing high-quality education and less preoccupied with students' health and behavioural needs.
2. Facilities that provide an enriched educational experience but also address children's psychological and behavioural needs to meet these ends.
3. Facilities focused on meeting an identified cognitive or educational deficit in children's development. Since such deficits frequently have their origins in family dysfunction and/or are manifest in poor behaviour of the child, the placement demands considerable specialist resources.
4. Facilities for children with a mixture of social, psychological and behavioural needs and those who are generally educated in ordinary schools; the placement tends to be short and part of a range of provision focused on several family members, not just the child.
5. Facilities for children with serious psychological needs and behavioural problems that overshadow other developmental goals, including education; some of these placements are secure.

The classification can be understood as a continuum, with placements that are primarily focused on the child's education at one end, and those primarily focused on the child's behaviour at the other. It is worth noting that the types of establishments have relevance for staff training, which is discussed later. For example, a 'social pedagogy' model has a far broader notion of education than the traditional one.

A strong influence on where a home or school lies on this continuum is parental involvement and autonomy over decisions regarding the child's care. In the first category, parents tend to be highly involved, possibly explaining the relatively low amount of investment in questions regarding behaviour. Parents are 'purchasing' or agreeing to an education for their child and expect to be highly involved in alterations to plans agreed at the point of reception. In the second category, parental involvement and autonomy tend to be diluted, sometimes reflecting their inability to pay for the provision. In the gap created by parents, professional autonomy is increased and attention to behaviour and other needs rises accordingly.

As most residential provision for children has dual or triple functions, this classification should help placements to locate themselves alongside similar provision operating in other sectors. Many residential schools for example have, by this classification, more in common with some child welfare placements than with schools that are narrowly focused on education. Thus, the focus on children's needs and approaches to meet them is emphasised at the expense of administrative categories based on single presenting problems.

MODELS OF RESIDENTIAL WORK WITH CHILDREN

There are many models and schools of thought surrounding residential care for children. Eight such approaches will now be discussed.

Procedural approaches

A number of texts address the residential task as if it were primarily a logistical task. These writers produce voluminous collections of guidance and advice as to how things 'should be done'. However, although the specific advice itself may be perfectly valid, the exhortatory and often atheoretical tone of the writing soon becomes wearying to the reader. Thus Kahan (1995) has 374 pages of advice, broken down into subheadings such as 'do not gloss over the evident concerns in the hope that they will go away when the child has settled in' (p. 113). Likewise Davison (1995) contains over 400 pages of advice and guidance to practitioners although, like Kahan, much of this advice, while unobjectionable, is articulated more in terms of 'common sense' and proceduralism than as a theoretically based approach to a professional task.

Authors such as these often themselves quote extensively from governmental guidance, and the work frequently has a worthy though unsophisticated feel. Similar texts have been produced by quasi-governmental and often short-lived advisory groups. One of the more productive and constructive of these was the Support Force for Residential Care, which issued a string of useful publications including *Good Care Matters* (1995). Despite (or perhaps because of) their relative lack of clearly articulated theory, such publications have often been welcomed by local authority training departments as the basis for short courses and training days for residential staff on specific themes. However, the risk in following this approach too closely is that staff (often unqualified) will be told what to do without understanding why they are doing it.

Psycho-social theory

At the other end of the spectrum there is a range of theoretical material which might broadly be characterised as drawing on a 'psycho-social' perspective, in other words combining a psychological understanding of the experience of care from the point of view of child, family and carers with a 'social' understanding of the context within which these relationships are provided. These take several forms.

Psychodynamic and therapeutic

Many of the early writings on residential child care came from within this approach, including the psychodynamic and explicitly therapeutic work of Beedell, Balbernie and Dockar-Drysdale. Later work from within the therapeutic perspective includes the therapeutic community approach (Rose 1990 and 1997; Ward and others 2003). These texts typically focus on the fine detail of children's emotional needs and on ways of addressing them using both individual and group methods and stressing the importance of the overall environment in which care and treatment are provided. An important addition to this literature was Jim Rose's book on *Working with Young People in Secure Accommodation* (2002), which explores the application of a similar approach to the 'secure' task.

To a large extent the 'pure' psychodynamic approach has remained within the more specialised therapeutic communities, although some of the principles and methods have percolated further into the mainstream. In addition, a very small proportion of children in 'ordinary' children's homes may have access to externally-provided psychotherapy (Boston and Szur 1983; Hunter 2001), although it is evident from Berridge's review that, while the majority of young people in the care system may have great emotional need, in most cases very little direct or specialist help is provided to meet it.

Therapeutic care versus 'ordinary mainstream child care'

Insofar as there is useful theory for residential carers, a significant proportion of it tends to originate in the field of therapeutic care, where experienced practitioners, often from a psychotherapeutic background, have described their work with children with varying degrees of emotional disturbance. This work provides a language for the complex emotional problems of the children and for the types of care and treatment which they need, albeit in a language that is sometimes experienced by mainstream practitioners as too specialised and even obscure. Nevertheless if it is true that a very high proportion of looked after children have mental health problems, then the understandings of the therapeutic perspective should be of value across the board. It is perhaps significant that one of the most positive units described in Brown and colleagues' 1998 study of structure and outcomes was a unit of a therapeutic community.

There is sometimes a reluctance in the management of local authority 'ordinary children's homes' to think in terms of therapeutic care. This reluctance may be due to anxiety that therapeutic care will require much greater skills and depth of knowledge than 'ordinary care'; there may be a feeling that the children in 'ordinary' children's homes are not in need of therapeutic support but simply require ordinary 'common sense' caring; or there may be a view that therapeutically oriented care would not support children's family links, rights, cultural and ethnic identity, and will not address the poverty and oppression of their lives. The therapeutic approach is thus seen by some as irrelevant and inappropriate for many children. Indeed most children probably do not need *therapeutic community* type of care, but it can certainly be argued that all those coming into residential care even for a brief period deserve to be treated with respect, care and understanding, and are likely to need skilled personal support during what is by definition a crisis point in their lives. One task for those engaging with the theory is to extract the transferable aspects of the therapeutic approach into the mainstream settings.

Attachment theory

Attachment theory may be seen as a development or parallel path of the psychodynamic approach, since both use 'inner world' perspectives to explain people's relationships and psycho-social needs. Much contemporary social work literature (for example, Howe 1995), including work on foster care, draws upon attachment theory, although this approach has been surprisingly slow to be applied fully in the residential setting. Two texts that have begun to do so are Fahlberg (1990) and Cairns (2002); the latter focusing more on her experience as a long-term foster carer though with clear implications for residential staff.

Other approaches to emotional need

Other work has focused on individual children's emotional needs and how this can be responded to in the residential context, though without using an explicitly psychodynamic or attachment-theory lens. A noteworthy recent addition to this literature is Anglin's (2002) 'grounded theory' study of 10 residential units in Canada, which draws attention to the central task of the staff of 'responding to pain and pain-based behaviour' in the children. Anglin's work is useful in connecting this theme of the emotional challenge facing the staff within a wider context: a) the overall task of the homes of 'providing an extrafamilial living environment'; b) the goal of the residents of 'developing a sense of normality'; and in particular, c) in locating the whole enterprise within a core theme of the 'struggle for congruence' in service of the children's best interests. This core theme echoes UK research findings on the importance of 'organised and consistent ways of working' (SSI 1993) and on the need for congruence between different stakeholders' objectives for homes.

Systemic approaches

A significant contribution to the understanding of the residential task was made by Miller and Gwynne (1972) using an 'open systems' model to explore the connections between task and method, input and output. Their focus is on the 'primary task', defined as the task that the organisation 'must perform in order to survive'. In addition they examine the anxieties that the task entails, in terms of the often unacknowledged demands that society makes of the homes and that may impinge directly on staff's ability to engage with the emotional demands of the work. Systemic approaches have also been applied to the detail of everyday work with young people in the group care setting (Ward 2002). Burton (1998) also includes a useful discussion of the primary task. The systemic approach offers a useful framework for managers and staff consultants when exploring the congruence of aims and methods in practice.

The use of groups and groupings

A central theme in residential care is that both young people and staff are living and working in groups: the argument is that, for the care to be positive and successful, considerable skill and understanding is required in both formal and informal groupwork on the part of the carers. Brown and Clough (1989) outline the concept of 'groups and groupings' to describe the ways in which work with informal groupings in everyday life contributes to the performance of the residential task. Their book includes a number of papers by practitioners and academics describing applications of this approach in a range of group care settings, including residential child care. This theme has been underexplored in more recent literature, although Emond (2002) highlighted the positive significance for young people of the resident group. Indeed, if the move in policy towards smaller and smaller homes of one and two children were to become the norm, the 'group' element of group care has little relevance. In addition, groups of residents are increasingly viewed as offering risk rather than opportunity for children.

Focus on family inclusion

The vital question of children's links with their families has also been under-represented in the residential child care literature until recently, a gap which has probably both reflected and contributed to the relative lack of attention given to this area in much earlier residential practice. Chakrabarti and Hill's collection (2000) includes several significant contributions on children's links with their families and peers, most notably a review article by Hill (2000). Ainsworth (1997) proposed a model of *Family Centred Group Care* for children, based upon the case study of a single institution in Australia.

It is worth noting in passing that Chakrabarti and Hill's important collection emerged from a major conference at the Scottish Institute for Residential Child Care (SIRCC) in 1996 – one indication of the many ways in which such a centre may provide a focus and stimulus for the production of more useful theory and thus of better practice.

Hill (2000) reviews the importance to both children and families of sustaining and supporting contact between them, and reviews the existing literature on residential care, finding that many earlier texts (in the 1970s and 1980s) made scant reference to such contact. He argues for a more inclusive conceptualisation of the residential task, aiming, in Ainsworth's words, 'to preserve and, wherever possible, to strengthen connections between children in placement and their birth parents and family members' (Ainsworth 1997, p. 35). This argument is well supported by research findings (for example, Millham and others 1986), which confirm that children who are enabled to maintain and develop such contact are likely to have better outcomes than those whose contact is much less.

On the other hand, while this model will work well for the majority of young people, it will not work well for all. Hill (2000) and Sinclair and Gibbs (1998) all acknowledge that for a minority of children family contact may be much more problematic and in some cases downright dangerous for children, especially where there is a risk of continuing abuse. In these cases the task of residential staff in relation to children's families of origin is less one of facilitating contact and more one of helping the children to understand and recover from what has happened to them, and learn how to live with little or no contact.

Since many children have lived in rapidly changing family circumstances and/or have endured multiple moves through several substitute families before even entering residential care, the question of family contact is further complicated. For example, there may be several families or parts of families with whom the child might wish to have contact, including former foster carers and adoptive parents as well as different 'wings' and generations of their family of origin, plus different siblings who may themselves be placed in substitute families or other residential settings. Here the challenge is one of enabling the child to make sense of and maintain (sometimes selective) contact with an extensive network of contacts rather than with one original parental home. It might still be argued that the task here is one of 'inclusion', although what is being included may be an acknowledgement and understanding of earlier trauma and continuing risk, rather than active contact.

For practitioners and managers, the theme of family contact might be summarised in terms of 'working with the family in mind', which may mean very different things for different children. The essential requirement on staff will be that they do keep the family in mind and that they provide the child with active support and encouragement to do so (Pooley 2003).

Meeting socio-political concerns

The social-political context in which residential care is delivered is addressed by Frost, Mills and Stein (1999), who take the empowerment of young people as their central theme. They propose a model for future practice based on clarity of purpose in each unit, with small residential units as an integral part of a wider child care system, itself based on an ethos of support and prevention. This model takes a different approach from the 'therapeutic' model, although it might be argued that from the child's point of view 'empowerment' might feel more similar to 'therapy' than either school of thought might expect to be the case. Baldwin (1990) claims, as do many others such as Menzies Lyth (1997) and Clough (2000), that there is a direct connection between the extent to which residential staff themselves feel informed and empowered (especially in relation to decision-making about the children) and their ability in turn to provide empowering care to young people.

Ensuring a positive role in welfare systems

A significant body of work has analysed residential services within the structural context of child care and other welfare services, and proposed a sociological analysis of the operation, both of regimes as a whole and of structures, cultures and subcultures within these regimes.

Some researchers adopting this perspective have expanded this approach to theorise about residential care more broadly. Their texts tend to emphasise what there is in common between residential care with different groups and in different contexts, including similarities with daycare and other services, and overlaps as well as contrasts with other forms of social work and social care. The focus of this approach tends to be on the interaction between the care career of the individual client and the operation of the group-living system in the home (Burton 1993; Clough 2000; Ward 2006).

Ensuring ethical standards

Finally, it is important to note that Stanley and Reed (1999) analysed residential institutions in terms of 'ethical audit' and developed a model aimed at preventing abuse and neglect and promoting general welfare in institutions.

In concluding this discussion of models of residential work with children, it is worth reiterating that no single theory of child behaviour or residential practice provides all the answers:

> in an area of human affairs so complex, no single comprehensive theory is possible: many different perspectives are relevant and should be considered complementary'.
> (Bullock, Little and Millham 1993, p. 19).

CONDITIONS FOR EFFECTIVE PRACTICE

When looking at residential establishments for children, the immediate reference points are the surface features, such as the style of leadership, the fabric and resources. Judgements about quality are often reached from immediate experiences, initial conversations with staff or the visible responses of the children. It is easy to assume that the most important aspects are either the people or the regime and that, if these elements are right, all will be well. But a stream of research into this area has revealed a more complicated situation.

Certainly, individuals, whether an efficient manager or an unruly adolescent, are important in affecting what happens in a home or school but they are not enough to explain everything. Successful managers in one context often fail elsewhere and establishments vary in their capability to help young people. Some features that common sense might associate with a good home have been found to be relatively insignificant. The qualities of buildings, the proportion of trained staff, the characteristics of the children, for example, are not sufficient *on their own* to produce good results.

We look next therefore at seven aspects of residential settings identified in the research studies in order to assess their significance for establishing good quality homes and achieving optimal outcomes for children and families.

The culture of residential establishments

While residential homes have many aspects that can be easily differentiated, such as buildings, staff roles or types of children, there is something extra – something more than the sum of the parts – that seems to be important in determining what happens therein. Many writers have used terms such as 'culture' or 'ethos' to describe this. It is precisely these feelings and messages that a visitor picks up. They may be long-standing, such as when there is a traditional way of doing things, or may be a product of stress or boredom. These cultures have been shown by research to be especially important because they directly affect the behaviour of children and staff, not just in terms of conformity or deviance but also in shaping attitudes.

The inheritance from early studies of residential care is a number of clear messages for policy and practice. Regimes have a considerable effect on children's behaviour while they are resident, and welfare-oriented approaches have consistently been found to produce better results than other approaches for children's health, education and personal social development. Staff and child cultures have long been known to influence outcomes even if the precise nature and direction of the association has been difficult to determine. The principal conclusion from this evidence was that managers should ensure that cultures did not cohere in a negative and destructive way.

But the usefulness of these findings for managers and staff charged with making residential care work has been limited. Even homes seemingly well planned from the start have failed to succeed. A list of correlations between structural variables and outcomes is difficult for managers to interpret, especially when the message is more a case of what should not happen than a clear indication of what needs to be done. Nor are global descriptions, such as the notion of a 'good home' or putting together a 'positive culture', of much value in the mêlée of daily residential life. It has not helped that many research messages were fashioned prior to the Children Act, 1989 which sets out a framework for the care of children and views the role of residential care in the context of a continuum of services for all children in need. As in life itself, everything in residential care can seem to be related to everything else, and emphasising single features can stifle rational discussion. How many times has the tautology 'a good home is one which has a good manager' or 'a good home is one which is a happy home' been heard?

Several large-scale empirical studies have studied this in detail and help us understand better how residential establishments work: *Working in Children's Homes: Challenges and complexities* (Whitaker, Archer and Hicks 1998); *Children's Homes: A study in diversity* (Sinclair and Gibbs 1998) and *Making Residential Care Work: Structure and culture in children's homes* (Brown and others 1998). The first takes a relatively unusual starting point of the experiences of staff; the second analyses the factors that predict optimal outcomes, and the third looks at the relationship between staff and child cultures, to unravel precisely what causes what.

The staff cultures described in the first book had much in common in that they espoused the same overall goal of benefiting the young people, faced the same range of tasks and shared many of the same values. Yet each was unique with respect to the details of its beliefs and attitudes, rules of behaviour, procedures, routines and customs, degree of internal cohesiveness and the nature of the boundary between the home and the outside world. Hence, some staff groups were mutually supportive, some were conflict ridden, some were secure and competent, and others were not.

The distinctive cultures that emerged in each case were influenced by the specific circumstances that staff faced. Key influences were:

- rate of turnover of the young people
- proportion of emergency placements
- mix of young people
- number of young people not in school
- stability of membership in the staff group
- composition of both young people and staff with respect to ethnicity and gender
- feelings of security among staff within their own organisation
- presence or absence of conflict with managers
- level of morale.

The second book, *Children's Homes: A study in diversity*, charted variations in the immediate and long-term outcomes of the 48 homes studied in order to explain the variation in outcomes in terms of the characteristics of residents, structural features of the homes and regimes adopted.

It was found that the background features of the children did not explain the wide variations in such outcomes as young people's offending behaviour and absconding. Difficult social environments in the homes were not related to previous difficult behaviour by residents or to levels of staff training.

The residents judged homes according to whether they wanted to be there, whether there was a purpose to their stay, whether they moved on at the right time and the quality of life on leaving. A third did not want to be in care at all. The young people appreciated homes:

- if they were not bullied, sexually harassed or led into trouble
- if staff listened, the regime was benign and the other children friendly
- if they showed some tangible improvement, such as in education.

Most wanted contact with their families but not necessarily to live with them.

In conclusion, Sinclair and Gibbs found that homes did best if:

- they were small
- the head of the home felt that his or her role was clear, mutually compatible, not disturbed by reorganisation and that he or she had autonomy
- staff agreed on how the home should be run.

When the outcomes for the children were assessed, it was found that individual misery was related to sexual harassment, bullying, missing family and friends, poor relations with other residents and lack of success in esteemed roles such as sport.

The connection between regime and outcomes for children was that young people adjusted better socially if, first, the head of the home had a clear idea of the ways in which aims were to be achieved, and second, staff turnover was not high.

Although this study is restricted to children's homes, it has several policy implications. These are that:

- children's homes should be kept small
- heads should be appointed only if they have a clear philosophy, agree with management on how the home should be run, are sensitive to the needs and wishes of residents and can unite the staff group

- contact between children and families should be encouraged while acknowledging that many residents do not want to live at home
- high staff to child ratios and high levels of staff qualification are not sufficient conditions for successful work in residential settings
- the work complementing residential care is important; emphasis might be put on adequate preventive work before admission, an ability to handle discharge at the residents' own pace and providing adequate aftercare.

The focus of the third book, *Making Residential Care Work: Structure and culture in children's homes*, is the relationship between the structure of homes and the staff and child cultures within them. *Making Residential Care Work* seeks to take thinking forward in several ways.

First, it sets out a linear model of cause and effect. It argues that, in children's homes at least, the structure of the home determines the staff culture; the staff culture determines the child culture, which, in turn, determines outcome for homes and for children. While there is obviously some feedback in the process, the model is able to discount the possibility of the opposite situation where cultures determine structures. Structure is defined as 'the orderly arrangements of social relations and a continuing arrangement of kinds of people governed by a concept of proper behaviour in their relations with each other'. Culture is defined 'as a quality discernible in response to a problem encountered by a group'.

The second contribution is the focus on the homes themselves and the ways in which they change. Change, like all other components in the model, has good and bad effects, encouraging improvements in the better homes but exacerbating difficulties elsewhere. Change in itself is not sufficient to lift standards in the poorer homes although, self-evidently, it is necessary to improve practice. Without knowing its effects or what it is supposed to achieve, much innovation is wasted. The difficulty is knowing where in the chain of effects to intervene. Is it best to empty a bad home and start again, or is more training or a new leader the answer?

Given these perspectives, the recommended starting point is the three different types of goals that homes pursue. These are defined as:

- societal
- formal
- belief.

Societal goals are those implied by law or expectation; formal goals are the representation of societal goals in local management practice; and belief goals reflect the underlying values of managers and staff.

The study argues that it is the relationship between these three types of goals that forms the basis of the structure of the home. Thus, if goals are out of balance or the relationship is contradictory, no amount of work on staff and child cultures will improve the situation. The book goes on to posit a model in which structures are seen to influence staff cultures, which, in turn, influence child cultures.

Generally this relationship appears to hold, although some of the links were not quite as direct as just described. For example, the strength of cultures differed, as measured according to the extent to which behaviour in a range of situations is controlled. The effects of these cultures also varied; the values they supported reinforced the goals of the homes in some cases but not others. Child cultures, in contrast, were less evident. Rarely were they strong and positive, in four of the nine homes studied they existed but were weak, and in three more they were hardly apparent. This latter situation probably reflects the variety of children's past experiences, their isolation from peers and the small size of the living groups.

In children's homes, therefore, strong cultures are not necessarily bad. Indeed, staff can benefit from the insights and practical help offered by positive peer support, and managers can use this strength, along with training and supervision, to further the work of the home. Child cultures are more difficult to manage, but a strong culture can complement the work of staff provided children implicitly understand the goals of the establishment, comprehend the way their particular home implements these, and perceive senior staff as people able to achieve something on their behalf. In such situations, there is no need to fragment the child culture. Thus, a hardy annual of residential care theory is modified in the light of new evidence.

How does this study help overcome the tautology that a good home is a home that is good? To do this, outcomes were assessed both for the homes themselves and for the children. When these indicators were applied, it was clear that homes that did best on nearly all the criteria employed were those with concordant goals, strong positive staff cultures, and either strong positive child cultures or ones that were fragmented without undermining the work of the establishment. On nearly all the measures used to assess outcomes for young people, while some children did better than others, they all did best in the better homes. Thus the final link in the explanatory model is completed.

All of these studies emphasise that when children are looked after, there is a danger that deficiencies in the care placements will exacerbate the deprivation and harm that necessitated the initial separation from family. A child doing badly in residential care needs a good-quality intervention, not transfer to another poor-quality home. System neglect, whereby the needs of children remain unmet, is less obvious than physical or sexual abuse but is no less dangerous. So how can the situation be improved?

- There is little benefit in looking at homes in isolation. There may be organisational changes that may improve situations, such as better record keeping or more effective communication, but this is unlikely to be sufficient to lift a home out of the doldrums or guarantee high standards.
- There has to be an understanding of the needs of the children being looked after in the home. This was not common among the homes studied, resulting in opinionated generalisations about children's situations and limited action in areas such as health, education and work with families.
- There also has to be an awareness of how residence is one of many means of meeting the child's needs. An appropriate package of services, shown by research to be the most effective known, has to be compiled.

Quality of relationships between children and carers

It is not surprising that the quality of the relationship between adult carer and child is frequently cited as a key factor in successful practice in both fostering and residential care. Sinclair and Gibbs (1998) report that children's sense of well-being was influenced most by how they got on with fellow residents. However, they note that, as by most measures staff were considered good or caring, there was little to separate homes in this respect. Other studies give greater weight to the impact of staff.

Relationships do not exist in a vacuum: they are influenced by, and in turn influence, the environment in which children live. Daily life must be built around the best interests of the children. Clough (2000) quotes from Parker's summary of research:

> Parker (1988) notes the information from various studies that different regimes have differential effect on children's behaviour: the best results are achieved by child-orientated rather than institution-orientated practices.

> [In] ... retrospective accounts provided by adults and young people who had been in care it is the sense of receiving understanding, sympathetic, comforting and individual attention which stands out as the hallmark of the experiences which they cherish. (p. 111)

> Establishments do 'best' when the children feel they are cared for, listened to and responded to in a quiet, sympathetic, and consistent fashion. (p. 115)

Clough (2000, pp. 88–90) then sets out factors he contends are intrinsic to resident-centred practice:

- The starting point is an attempt to understand the resident: this is an active search.
- The daily life within the home is built from an attempt to produce systems that best match residents' wants and needs.
- There is time within the daily routine to listen to individual residents.
- Residents are involved in negotiations about life in the establishment.
- Staff worry about residents: they are concerned for residents, hold on to their interests and continue to think about what will work best for them, even when they are not with residents.
- Residents must feel that they are at the centre of life in the home, that their interests and well-being matter to staff.
- The key to good experience for the residents is that they feel they matter, that they are cared for and cared about.
- In effect, the experience of the resident should be at the heart of practice.

Whitaker, Archer and Hicks (1998, p. 170) echo these sentiments, stating that good practice includes:

- being ready to listen, both to the evidently momentous and to the apparently mundane

■ being sensitive to a young person's readiness, or not, to talk and to share feelings and experiences

■ combining non-verbal or symbolic forms of caring with verbal, explicit ones

■ noticing good or admirable behaviour and crediting a young person for it

■ marking special occasions in a young person's life with a celebration.

In a later study Berridge (2002, p. 92) sets out similar factors that his research suggests as characterising good relationships. The most effective staff in this respect:

■ are informal in approach, easy to talk to

■ respect young people, listen to what they say, try to understand and not lecture them

■ are frank and sometimes challenging, rather than 'pushy' and 'nagging'

■ are available, punctual and reliable

■ keep confidences

■ do practical things to help

■ keep their promises.

All of this recent work serves to refine the findings of earlier studies of residential child care. King, Raynes and Tizard, writing in 1973, compared hospital wards, children's homes and hostels for children with severe learning disabilities. They rated highest those where the children were accorded respect as individuals (p. 198). Although arguing that bringing up children in a child-oriented environment leads to improved performance by the children, they add a moral dimension: 'kindliness and consideration … seem to us important whether or not they benefit children in measurable terms' (p. 199).

However, it is essential to note, as do McNeish, Newman and Roberts (2002), that young people's experiences of adults (whether social workers, foster carers, residential staff or teachers) are hugely variable. Morris (2000) quotes from several children who had bad experiences of adults. She summarises this as: 'Some people who work with children don't like children. They disempower them and, at worst, abuse them' (p. 14).

Another aspect of the context in which relationships take place is whether the system allows them to endure, in contrast to situations where the adults choose to withdraw. Morris (2000, p. 7) discusses the regularity with which successful relationships in short-term fostering have to be broken in the search for a long-term home.

In addition to the importance of adult–child relationships in terms of quality of life and outcome, several writers point out that child-to-child relationships are also a core component of the child's world. In the last 15 years there has been increasing recognition of the fact that children can make life terrible for other children. Whitaker and colleagues (1998) found that staff were likely to think that children should be left to sort out their problems themselves, but in the process of children sorting out their problems, many young people were bullied. Cawson and colleagues (2001) confirm that young people still often perceive carers as not knowing about or not intervening in the verbal or other bullying that may occur, although a further publication from this team shows that more positive homes provide much more successful management of such problems (Barter and others 2004). The key factor seems to be to recognise the importance to children in terms of so much of daily living with other children, but not to think that the child's world can necessarily be left to look after itself.

It is relevant here to note that many people who would be seen as pioneers of therapeutic work, such as David Wills or George Lyward, would have expected both to get to know what was happening between children *and* to intervene in the children's worlds. Some would do this through group or community meetings, or in what Homer Lane in the early 1900s termed 'children's courts'. Lane set up a children's residential unit called the Little Commonwealth between 1913 and 1918, based on principles of what would later be termed shared responsibility. The processes were always the same: first, there were efforts to create environments in which children felt safe to talk about their experiences, including those that made them unhappy; second, all children had to understand the impact of their behaviour on the lives of others; third, the group membership was used as a means of overriding the authority that individual children may have usurped. At the heart of this approach was building a loyalty to a culture and a group, to the 'way we do things here'. The group was seen as having the potential for a positive impact, rather than, as so often today, a liability.

We have already noted that where there is a positive child culture, then there is less need for direct staff intervention: however, there are many occasions when it is important for staff to intervene in the child's world.

This is recognised also in the very different approaches of therapeutic communities: the staff have to plan the environment to hold and nurture both individual children *and* the group of children. In the process, such communities aim to find ways both to watch and to influence children's responses to one other.

Staffing and training

Impact of qualification

Despite the expected benefits of training for staff, Sinclair and Gibbs (1998) could find no evidence in their study of children's homes that either better-qualified staff or a higher ratio of staff to children in themselves predicted better outcomes for children. This is a disturbing finding given the emphasis that is repeatedly given in official guidance to the need for better-qualified staff.

Yet although the employment of qualified staff does not predict better outcomes, it is clear that the staff world is a very important factor in successful work. So what is the process? It may be that there is a certain level of training that is essential for good outcomes or that some other staff factors such as confidence, morale, culture and leadership are more influential than training. The conclusion seems to be that training is a necessary but not, on its own, a sufficient condition for good practice.

Two other factors may be relevant. The first is the consideration that the available training courses have not been appropriate to the task of working in residential homes, a view discussed more fully below.

The second is that staff have not been able to put their training into effect. There is some evidence to support this in that some staff do report not being able to work in the ways that they want (Hills and Child 1998). Sinclair and Gibbs note that it is possible qualified staff were more likely to have low morale because of the 'incongruence between their training and the job they found themselves doing' (p. 149).

Background

There are several other key aspects of the staffing of residential homes including selection and recruitment; qualification and training; and support and development. The overarching questions are:

- Which sort of people should work with children or, put another way, what makes a good residential worker?
- How do we select them?
- What training do they need?
- What are the conditions that will enable them to work well?
- How are these conditions to be created?

Beedell and Clough (1992, p. 1) in evidence to the *Inquiry into the Selection and Recruitment of Staff*, argued that the lack of theorising in residential work had an impact on the way the task was undertaken:

> Too often residential work is undertaken with no analysis of problems and no theoretical base for practice. The consequence is that staff may be ill equipped to do the job, and outsiders ... have no framework for examining what goes on.

Theory is little used to inform training (and thus practice). Aside from providing guidance, understanding and mastery of tasks and skills by individuals, which ought to contribute to better outcomes for children, training also operates at a broader or deeper but highly significant level. It should play a key role in the discovery by staff and young people of what actually works in practice in their own home and, indeed, could be influential in establishing the consensus about goals and methods that have been highlighted by the studies discussed as being central factors in good residential care, as well as in promoting in staff a curiosity about understanding their task more fully.

Of course, dangers might arise from casual theorising. As Utting warns, 'the development of institutionalised practices may lead to staff losing awareness that what they are doing constitutes a form of child abuse' (DH 1991, p. 36). This may well be the case where the practice arises from a new 'philosophy' or method of care which has not been exposed to external scrutiny. But this risk is no excuse for dismissing the significance of theoretical perspectives.

The discussion on staffing which follows must be located in the context of the understanding that there is of the task in residential care.

Current qualification and training

Professional qualifying training has not been widely available to residential workers since the demise of the certificate of social service

(CSS) programmes 20 years ago. More recently the introduction of NVQ, with requirements on local authorities to ensure that all care staff hold minimal levels of achievement, has led to a considerable increase in the amount of training provided to staff. It must always be remembered, however, that NVQ is not in itself a training programme, but a scheme for assessing people's abilities in tightly defined aspects of their existing work. Two commentators observe:

> NVQ is only a beginning and will never provide the sufficiently comprehensive approach implied in government policy.
> *(Crimmens and Pitts 2000, p. 92)*

While an NVQ may be used as a tool for implementing in-house training schemes, and gaining nationally recognised *vocational* awards, it should not be confused with a recognised *professional* qualification. Residential workers should have the same access to professional qualifications, including academic awards, as other groups of staff. We have already noted the high levels of psychiatric disorder of young people in residence. This being the case, the levels of skill required by the staff should not be underestimated. NVQs offer a reasonable introduction to the basics of the work, but need to be accompanied by a much more sophisticated programme of staff training and development.

The recognised professional qualification for working in residential child care has been a diploma in social work (DipSW), or one of its predecessors. Staff may gain some qualifications via an NVQ route. However, the UK is the only European country that sees social work as the core professional discipline for residential child care. Increasingly many in the UK have argued that, in spite of several attempts, social work training does not adequately prepare people for working in residential establishments and is not the proper professional base for residential practice. We agree with those who state that being embedded in social work training impacts on practice in residential homes and schools in two ways. First, too often it fails to equip staff for the work they have to do. Second, residential social workers with a generic field and residential qualification are more likely to move out of residential work than are field workers to move in.

As a result, a very small proportion of qualifying social workers opt to work in residential care, and social work courses have continued to be perceived by residential staff as insufficiently geared to their training needs, with (for example) very little focus on group living and group work, or on ways of handling issues arising in daily living. Exceptions to this pattern would be those few programmes that offer a 'residential pathway' for residential child care workers, of which the best known is probably the one at Strathclyde University associated with the Scottish Institute for Residential Child Care (SIRCC). The aim of the institute, wider than just qualification training, is:

> to ensure that residential child care staff throughout Scotland have access to the skills and knowledge they require to meet the needs of the children and young people in their care.
> *(SIRCC website)*

The social work qualification was relaunched as a degree programme in 2003, based in part upon the National Occupation Standards (NOS) of field social workers. Even though these NOS do include some focus on group care and groupwork issues, they are not the NOS of residential child care staff (which have yet to be drawn up), so it is inevitable that the new social work degree will perpetuate the mismatch with residential care of the old DipSW and Certificate of Qualification in Social Work (CQSW) courses. Learndirect, an organisation 'with a remit to provide high quality post-16 learning' sets out the current requirements for training for residential workers:

> As a residential social worker you may be encouraged to undertake a relevant NVQ/SVQ level 2 or 3 in Health and Social Care (formerly known as NVQ in Care). Within this qualification you can specialise in working with children and young people, or adults. Support workers can gain recognition for their level of expertise by working towards a foundation degree in a subject such as health and social care, or assisting professional practice. It is important to check the entry requirements with each institution; relevant work experience and vocational qualifications are highly regarded. On completion of the course, there is the potential to go onto year two of a degree programme leading to registration as a social worker. For career progression it may be necessary to become a qualified social worker, which will involve studying for an approved degree or postgraduate qualification in social work.
> *(Learndirect website, 2006)*

The National Occupational Standards for Managers in Residential Child Care were published in 2003 by Topss UK, and form the basis for the Registered Managers Award, which at the time of writing has had a relatively low take-up, being offered by about five or six centres in England.

An alternative route is the 'social pedagogy' model, variations of which are in use in many European countries. This model has been strongly advocated by a number of reports, including one from the Residential Forum (1998), but has yet to be implemented in any part of the United Kingdom. It is a model that focuses directly on understanding and addressing children's needs in their living situation, using a holistic approach, and taking account of the full range of services through which these needs may be met. It may therefore offer a much more focused and relevant framework for residential staff than the social work framework currently does, if adapted for a UK context from the other European contexts in which it has originated. The social pedagogy approach is among those being considered by the Children's Development Workforce on behalf of the DfES.

Characteristics of a good residential worker

Determining what is wanted in residential staff is a prerequisite to establishing sound selection procedures. What sort of experiences and capacities are wanted? Factors noted by Beedell and Clough (1992, p. 11) include:

> Fairly clear and acceptable motivation; capacity to engage with young people and with other adults; personal stability; some informed knowledge of the job and its demands; lack of refuge or power seeking.
>
> Is the person:
> - Concerned for children and young people? Does he or she LIKE them?
> - Can they play with and be comfortably alongside their entertainments?
> - Are they, at core, independent enough to withstand the batterings of children who are at the least adrift, and who may be very damaged and bewildered?
> - Can they serve as reasonable role models?

Despite the importance of these points, we are not aware of detailed studies of the characteristics of good practitioners in the residential field.

The staff worlds

Mainey (2004) in a study for the NCB reports that staff morale in residential child care is high. It is interesting that there were especially positive reports from staff in Northern Ireland, a country where there are high percentages of qualified staff. In ongoing work NCB is drawing together findings on the morale, qualifications and retention of staff across all four nations.

A summary of findings to date includes:

- Three quarters of staff are 'satisfied' or 'more than satisfied' with their jobs and morale is high.
- Motivating factors are teamwork, children's progress, knowing there is support available and pride in their work.
- There is clear guidance and information for staff to carry out their work.
- Handovers are important.
- Staff are positive about management, they though would like internal managers to be more aware of what is happening in the home and external management to acknowledge the experience of staff who work directly with young people.
- Managers' top concerns are lack of resources, children's participation in education and children's general progress.
- Staff would like to see changes to work patterns as they impact upon personal commitments.
- Training was seen as essential by all; the common frustration was that there was lack of training on specific issues and staffing levels stopped them attending.

Cooper (2005), in research for the Children's Workforce Strategy, draws on information from the Audit Commission to outline the reasons staff gave for working in and for leaving residential child care. Positive comments included: 'to make a difference'; 'because it's interesting'; and 'what I always wanted to do.' These reasons sustain staff, who tend to remain in the workforce for up to 10 years. Most staff leave because of push factors: lack of recognition and status, levels of pay and cost of living, being poached for other jobs, loss of job satisfaction, and lack of managerial support. Keeping staff is as much about investment in the young people as in the staff themselves.

He calculates costs financially and emotionally:

> Turnover rates in the children's workforce are especially important compared to other sectors. This issue has a strong bearing on continuity of care: children and young people are particularly vulnerable to changes in relationships built up with adults. ... In addition to the disruption to care and the financial costs, managers also find rates higher than around

15% unmanageable, meaning that turnover presents a multi-faceted burden. Given that rates as high as 26% have been recorded for residential care staff, and that turnover rates in general are around 10 to 15%, managers are clearly facing difficult challenges. (p.11)

Recruitment and selection

Following the realisation of the abuse on occasions perpetrated by staff on the children in their care, considerable attention has been given to the devising of appropriate selection procedures. However, there is an earlier important stage, that of recruitment: do people want to work in residential homes? The attraction of jobs is dependent not only on pay but also on the standing of the activity. Residential work has suffered from the bad publicity consequent on repeated revelations of abuse, and possibly from the unsocial hours that are demanded and the sheer complexity and difficulty of the work. The rewards are insufficiently recognised. Good selection procedures without consideration of the overall recruitment of staff will not ensure good staff come into the work.

None of the above is to deny the importance of selection procedures that are both rigorous and designed to pick out people with skills appropriate for the work. It is imperative that procedures are followed, even when under pressure because of staff shortages. An overview of what is required is to be found in *Too Serious a Thing* (National Assembly for Wales 2002, pp. 89–90), which refers to the 1992 DH report, *Choosing with Care*. Further discussion can be found in Clough and McCoy (2000, pp. 49–51). In summary:

- There should be checks of people's identity and of their qualifications.
- References must be taken up prior to interview, and there should be telephone conversations between a member of the interviewing panel and the referee.
- Referees should be reminded of the importance of their statements.
- Procedures should be devised that allow selectors to get as good a picture as possible of the person undertaking the sort of work that is typical of the post for which they are applying.

Professional support and development

Professional support for residential staff is absolutely paramount if they are to be able to give of their best. This is especially true in the current circumstances, given the changing population of young people in residence, particularly the high incidence of disturbed behaviour and mental health problems.

In addition to the general positive impact of effective leadership, mechanisms for staff support should include:

- team meetings
- supervision
- consultancy
- training and professional qualification.

Care standards include expectations of frequency of supervision and staff meetings, although they tend to address frequency rather than the quality or relevance of the content of the sessions. For example, residential care of troubled young people is potentially a very stressful occupation, and supervision needs to address the human experience of the carers as much as checking that they have fulfilled their formal duties. There is a risk in the 'standardisation' of care that issues of quality and 'process' become lost in the bureaucratisation of the work. Increasing regulation, formal guidance and inspection means that the work of homes is more tightly controlled than it has ever been, and yet regulation sometimes appears unrelated to the quality of the experience as perceived by the young people and the staff.

The quality of team meetings will also depend upon the access that staff have to decision-making mechanisms in the system. Baldwin's research (1990) indicates clearly that in some areas the efforts of residential staff are undermined by their virtual exclusion from information channels and decision-making systems and meetings, and she argues that in these circumstances they therefore do not have the 'power to care' properly for the young people. Contributory factors include local authority management systems, especially the arrangements for the line management of homes, and the patterns of communication between field and residential staff (Whipp, Kirkpatrick and Kitchener 2005).

Training for management

An additional problem in many areas is the shortage of suitably qualified and experienced candidates for leadership roles in residential homes. Research evidence is very clear as to the positive influence on all aspects of the care experience of clear, knowledgeable and sensitive leadership. But the supply of such individuals is limited, especially given the few opportunities for professional training. The National Occupational Standards for Registered Managers of Children's Residential Services underpin the Registered Managers Award, although there has been limited implementation of this award, as noted above.

Leadership

If a salient feature of the studies discussed is the importance of 'culture' or 'ethos' for outcomes, whether for the home itself or for the young people who live there, it seems likely from the evidence that leadership is an important determinant of this. To explore this possibility further, researchers at the University of York (Hicks and others 2003) conducted a survey of children's homes, looking specifically at leadership, while Whipp and colleagues at the Cardiff Business School (2005) looked at leadership in terms of the external management of children's homes, an area frequently highlighted as deficient in inspections and abuse inquiries.

Both studies explored the concept of leadership in the context of overall management. Management, states Whipp and colleagues, implies 'a need to achieve some degree of control and co-ordination to meet goals' (p. 16). The York group expand this:

> in order to manage a children's home successfully, managers had to function as more than good administrators and supervisors of daily tasks operating from within fixed budgets. Children's homes managers have to keep their fingers on the pulses of their homes, build and develop their teams, and provide an example in terms of practice with young people. In short, the term manager denotes authority by referring to the most senior role in an executive hierarchy. Leadership, put simply, may be seen as denoting influence.
> *(Hicks and others 2003, p. 113)*

Both studies then seek to delineate the different tasks facing managers in residential child care. They stress that although managing a children's service in which residential provision plays a part is not the same as managing an individual establishment, both are riddled with contradictions and require more than overseeing a stable and predictable bureaucracy. In the former, the different demands of legislation and government guidance, politicians, finance officers and other parts of the wider children and family services have to be satisfied. In the latter a complex set of roles has to be performed.

Managers of homes are leaders in the sense that they have to supervise and develop a staff team offering therapeutic work, encourage relationships with children's schools and families, and satisfy their superiors in central bureaucracies. In undertaking this work, there are balances to be struck, between energising staff but not disempowering them, and between being sensitive to the needs of individual children whilst setting boundaries and controls for the group. There are also expectations to act as a role model to adolescents and sustain the work of the home through bad patches.

Thus, four features of a residential setting, as identified by Bullock, Little and Millham in 1993, have to be concordant if success is to be achieved. An effective establishment has to admit the right sort of children, operate a regime that best meets the needs of their residents, pursue good child care practice and be well run. Failure in any one of these areas will reduce success in others. So a manager who is a good administrator but little else is likely to fall short in three of the four areas.

After a review of the numerous theories of management and leadership, both research teams conclude that leadership is best understood in the context of a social role rather than a personal attribute or innate skill. This is because of the inescapable facts that good leaders in one situation frequently fail in others, and similar results can be achieved by different management styles. The York team found a mixture of internal and external influences on leadership, any of which could affect performance. External factors included the status of the post, clarity of role and function, ability to spend time in the unit, and autonomy and the quality of external support. Internal factors were experience with the team, ability to influence practice and an effective strategy for handling children's behaviour and ensuring their education. Successful leadership in terms of consistent and reflective practice rests on a combination of these factors.

The dominant leadership factor affecting outcomes was the concept of 'strategy' because this produced a chain of effects that generally worked for the good of the home. A clearly worked-out strategy for dealing with children's behaviour and education increased staff morale, and they then felt they received clearer and better guidance, with the result that the children behaved better. Young people also expressed more positive views about the social climate of the home and were seen by their social workers as functioning better. All of this was independent of the background characteristics of the residents.

With regard to effects on children's behaviour, a clear strategy robustly implemented also reduced the likelihood of young people being convicted of criminal offences and being excluded from school, but not of running away. The effects on children's wider well-being were more difficult to discern because of the influence of so many intervening variables. Young people's welfare was increased by a clear strategy but this only pertained while they were resident.

The perspective adopted by Whipp and colleagues was more focused on management, defined as a technical activity or process directed towards goals via control and coordination as methods. Several aspects of management were explored: child care strategy and its implementation, the management of child placement, the line management of homes, managing and developing staff, monitoring and controlling the service, and, the arrangements for acquiring placements external to the local authority.

The emerging picture was one of variability in all areas. While efforts were being made to improve the situation, all of this activity was taking place in an inauspicious context in which child care aims are complex and competing and have to be pursued in a professional bureaucracy displaying the same two features. Hence:

> the move to enhance management practices in the area of children's services have been uneven and uncontested. New forms of control have not been fully implemented. There has been little fundamental change in occupational cultures or in personnel management practices. (p. 183)

From their evidence, the Cardiff team proposed an optimal model for managing children's homes. It has three elements. The first is that it has an inclusive orientation to the problem of external management. This means encompassing not only the home and line manager but also all other stakeholders, such as residential staff, service managers and resource controllers, fieldworkers, senior managers, support staff, other professionals, inspectors and elected members. The second element concentrates on how the process of management operates. The external management of homes comprises six core elements, which are *strategic planning, placement decisions, line management, developing staff, monitoring and control* and *managing external placements.* 'It is the choices made and actions taken in these areas which facilitate or constrain how external management operates at the level of practice within the distinctive context of children's services' (p. 192). Finally, 'both the assumptions and practices of external management require exploration in terms of the extent to which they meet the requirements and standards set not just by legislation, the DfES and relevant professional bodies but also take account of recognised measures found across the management literature. In general, standards of management were found to vary in the homes studied with arrangements for monitoring performance and remedial intervention especially poor' (p. 192).

In drawing conclusions, the complications inherent in all discussions of leadership and management in residential child care surface to confound the arguments. The fundamental problem is that the 'clinical' interventions necessary to help children whose needs lead them to residential placements are by no means clear. The relationship between interventions and outcomes for children and families, especially if measured on child development criteria, are still relatively tenuous, even in therapeutic communities where treatment programmes are well articulated. While much has been written about good practice, it is mostly in terms of social care standards and administrative processes rather than the 'technology' used to help children and families. This dearth of validated interventions to meet particular needs means that views about the best ways of tackling the difficulties children present, such as hostile family relationships, challenging behaviour and the effects of poor parenting, are likely to be opinion as much as fact.

While it seems certain from the evidence presented that bad management exacerbates poor outcomes, in residential child care the opposite does not necessarily apply. Good management may not correlate with good outcomes, at least in terms of children's health and development, either because no proven 'technology' exists or because the contrast between the supportive care environment and life that follows in the outside world is so sharp. This is why the long-term results of much structural and process reform are often disappointing (Morpeth 2004).

Listening to children

Many texts on residential child care place strong emphasis on the importance of good quality experience in daily life, but there has been relatively little on the detail of how this should be provided, at least in the form of accessible and yet adequately theorised texts for practitioners and how the experience relates to the wishes of the resident children. Bettelheim (1950) emphasised the importance of the child's own understanding of and valuing of good experience in the detail of everyday life (for example, food, bathing, bedtimes), and other texts which have emphasised this include *The Other 23 Hours* (Trieschman, Whittaker and Brendtro 1969), *Daily Experience in Residential Life* (Berry 1975), *Healing Hurt Minds* (Rose 1990) and Carter (2003).

Some of this material relates to the planning and management of routine experience; there is also the question of the handling of the unplanned or unexpected, which may comprise a large proportion of the daily life of residents. Some approach this theme from the perspective of the management and control of behaviour, while others acknowledge that it is often in their responses to the everyday challenges of child care that staff help children to feel a sense of being understood and valued, and that some of the most useful opportunities for constructive or even therapeutic communication may arise. Ward has coined the term 'opportunity led work' (1996) to draw attention to this potential for positive communication in the handling of everyday experience. It is perhaps significant that Brown and colleagues (1998) seek to measure and describe the culture of residential homes by studying the way in which these sorts of everyday incidents and challenges are handled by the staff. The more positive cultures tend to be the ones in which staff are more considered, constructive and consistent in their responses.

Size of home

The issue of the optimal size of a residential unit is an important one, especially as the number of residents is dropping, to the point where residential units for two children or even one child are becoming common. There are widely divergent views on size of home. Sinclair and Gibbs's (1998) study leads to a clear statement that on the whole, it is better to keep the size of children's homes small: better outcomes were achieved by smaller homes. However, Chipenda-Dansokho and colleagues (2003) claim that this is the only major study providing evidence in support of smaller units, and argue that a 'model that considers size in the context of institutional aims and structures is ...

a more fruitful approach to understanding the significance of size in service development'.

Very small residential homes are extremely costly to staff and seem to emulate some of the characteristics of a foster home without the key factors that make a foster home akin to a family setting: the fact that foster parents share the home with the child and do not go on and off duty. In small homes each child has far greater potential to disrupt the stability of life in the residential home, and produce a situation in which much of what happens is a direct response to his or her own behaviour.

Further, a small home denies the potential for children to be supportive to others in groups (Emond 2005). To counter this point, it must be recognised that there has been limited evidence from recent research of the benefits for children of interaction with others, and considerable evidence of damage from bullying and abuse. Whether this reflects a style of residential practice in which there has been little attempt to work with the group, 'to fragment a negative peer culture', has not been demonstrated.

Certainly there have to be searching questions as to whether enough is known about, first, good residential work with groups and, second, outcomes from fostering. Some have asserted that the negative aspects of fostering have yet to be studied. It may be that the closer living style in foster families reduces the likelihood of bullying and abuse, but we cannot yet be confident that this is the case.

Information recording and sharing

Better outcomes will be achieved if information about children looked after and their families is properly communicated to all those involved. This can be used to predict outcomes in all areas of the child's life, an exercise likely to encourage realistic expectations about the future and help tailor the intervention to the specific needs of each child.

Information about individual children can be aggregated to establish a picture in a single home, an area within a social services department, or across an entire local or health authority. Policy and practice developments should reflect such evidence. Information on children in need, particularly those looked after away from home, should also be used to ensure a workable fit between children placed in the same setting.

Furthermore, it goes without saying that information must be shared when appropriate between agencies, in particular with health and education.

CONCLUSIONS ON WHAT WORKS IN RESIDENTIAL PRACTICE

What authoritative findings can be drawn with regard to the relationship between the various factors of residential establishments that have been discussed? The Department of Health's (1998) research review *Looking After Children Away from Home*, along with the more recent publications discussed, have highlighted the conditions auspicious for effective residential work. The scientific status of these findings is variable, but there is sufficient evidence to show that outcomes for children and families and for homes themselves will be better if they are present. They cover a range of issues from the quality of information, creating good regimes, organisational features, such as optimal size and staffing, and the structure of the wider children and family services in which homes function.

It seems from the evidence that optimal results will be obtained if:

■ there is a strategic role for residential care in the wider children and family service
■ the expectations of residential care are realistic
■ residential care is viewed as meeting some of the needs of the young people and families, along with other services, at particular stages of a child's development
■ there is a care plan for the child that is based on his or her needs and harnesses services known to be the most likely to meet them
■ societal, formal and belief goals are concordant.

The aspects of effective management and leadership for individual homes are that:

■ the manager feels in control and supported
■ he or she has a clear strategy to make the home child-oriented
■ he or she delivers interventions to children and families that are the most logical and evidenced-based to meet their needs
■ he or she develops a staff team to implement these plans
■ he or she can sustain the approach through difficult periods
■ the home is small, or good practice is not prevented by the size of the establishments.

At a practice level, these aspects will be manifest in features of daily life in the home, such as:

- appropriate contact with family members
- involvement of children and, as appropriate, parents in decisions about their lives
- children being treated with respect
- children having the same access to education, health, employment and leisure as their peers
- children having access to the special services they may need
- a reduction in the aspects of behaviour that are known to be poor indicators for a child's development
- children being supported on leaving the home both in practical skills and in coping with potential loneliness and insecurity.

Yet as we seek to understand better the needs of children and families and react sensitively to them, we are faced with complexity and doubt. It is hard to separate the necessary and sufficient conditions or to know what comes before what in effective practice. Moreover, we know scarcely anything about the effects of residential work on child development (Little, Kohm and Thompson 2005). Take as an example leadership and management; these are undoubtedly important and without them we are unlikely to meet children's needs, no matter how well meaning our efforts. But leadership and management are only means to ends. The task, whether planning a comprehensive children's service or making a care plan for a child, is to identify needs, set desired outcomes in different areas of children's lives, and put in place the services most likely to achieve them. It is at that point that management and organisational issues come to the fore, but sadly, management is often the starting point for planning.

There are, of course, many other ingredients of high-quality residential care and more detail could be provided, for example with regard to the appointment procedures and support mechanisms for heads of homes, and the value of replacement managers with a track record of turning around failing homes. Similarly, residential staff have broad-ranging responsibilities. It is important to have mechanisms that encourage staff to keep sight of their principal responsibility, the priorities for the child and the home and cooperation with other professionals. Terms of employment should extend to their authority and autonomy to influence decisions concerning children in their care.

Morris (2000, p. 45) reported on the views of field social workers and residential care workers of what helped them to do their jobs properly. They included:

- being valued for their strengths
- being supported in the areas of their work that they found difficult
- good, regular supervision that is recorded and action taken when required
- realistic caseloads
- high-quality ongoing training and other resources, such as access to a library
- contact with good practice initiatives by other agencies.

Effective channels of communication in residential homes will also enable the staff to do their job well. Managers need to be kept informed about what staff discover in their day-to-day involvement with the children, and front line workers need to keep up to date with a manager's strategic thinking. Similarly, there are many benefits from inter-agency collaboration. For example, child protection services in local and health authorities could usefully introduce advice about the care of sexually abused and abusing children to policy and practice.

It also seems sensible to monitor the cultural response of the home. Homes should do those things (for example, joint training and development) that promote staff unity and avoid those (change of function, joining two teams, frequent use of temporary staff) that tend to be disruptive.

One matter that is of central concern in the development of residential services is the consideration of how to establish what we have set out from research findings as core characteristics of successful residential care. From research we know the factors that need to be in place but not how to ensure their existence. We repeat the core areas for consideration:

- ensuring goals are in harmony
- establishing the structure of the home
- establishing clear and coherent leadership
- establishing well articulated objectives, consistent through the organisation
- staff feeling that they have significant responsibility for life within the home
- creating structures for local authorities to act corporately.

What is important is that the first five of these lie within the remit of the children's services department; they cannot be established by residential homes on their own. Drawing on the DH research overview (1998), we set out five suggestions for the development of such a departmental strategy that will impact positively on practice.

More rigorous planning

Children in need, especially those looked after, might be better served if professionals were to set out attainable outcomes in all aspects of a child's life in relation to a selection of moments that seemed meaningful to the child and family alike. Questions should focus on where, and with whom, children are likely to live, as well as about their education, health and social relations. From the responses it should be possible to see how residence and other services can contribute to good outcomes – as distinct from considering what outcomes can be salvaged from the residential context. Alongside this, what is needed is a more sophisticated assessment of children's emotional and psychological needs in order to inform the planning process.

Early intervention

Looking for signs of later difficulty in an adolescent's life can be viewed as 'early intervention'. Looking for signals pointing to running away, delinquency, drug misuse or significant relationship problems in the years that follow entry to care or accommodation are to be encouraged. Once again, this is dependent upon accurate assessment of needs.

Inter-agency collaboration

Children in need would benefit if local authorities were to specify a joint policy at all levels in the organisation concerning the relationship between social services, health, education and other agencies.

Monitoring systems

Senior managers of children's services should know how many children they are looking after and where. By virtue of their characteristics, some of these children are likely to be missing temporarily, and special concern should be expressed about their well-being. It is not realistic to expect children never to run away. It is realistic to expect to know who is away, for how long, from where and why.

A service development perspective

Shifting the balance from inspection towards procedures that encourage the continuous improvement of services could be a more effective route to better quality and value. Effective monitoring and regulations are as likely to be achieved through good supervision, better training and good use of management information as through the attentions of a detached regulatory framework.

What does all this knowledge from research indicate as the best way forward for improving residential care? The research suggests three key aspects:

1. The policy and practice recommendations suggested by the researchers should be implemented immediately.
2. It encourages agencies to consider working towards providing a service that displays the characteristics of good homes (there would need to be further clarification of what such characteristics are).
3. It offers a systematic framework for radical change. This approach would start with a consideration of the needs of the children and how residential experiences can help meet them. The next stage would be to be clear about the aims and objectives of each home by setting reasonable and acceptable outcomes for the resident children. This would be followed by the development of structures in the homes that would best achieve these outcomes, thus ensuring that they operate effectively by developing staff skills and generating positive cultures.

The fundamental requirement for an effective service is that different types of goals are as congruent as possible. However, this abstract state needs to be underpinned by sound professional knowledge, appropriate processes and the good practice that the research studies have identified. In this overview we have sought not only to draw all the evidence together but also to extend the list for the various aspects of residential work with children and discuss contentious topics.

3 Planning residential services for children: a case study

THE BACKGROUND: THE REALITY OF CHILDREN'S EXPERIENCES AND THE REPORTS ON LOCAL PRACTICE

This review arose from the National Assembly for Wales commissioning work to inform the development of children's services in Wales. In this section we draw heavily on that material to illustrate the ways in which the evidence base of what works in residential care for children can be linked to the planning of services. Some of the material is general; other parts are specific to Wales.

Children's experiences

The planning of children's services ought to start from an understanding and recognition of the reality of the experiences of children and their families. The reality is that their lives are lived within conditions of immense personal pressure and turmoil; when things break down they do so with considerable force, creating confusion, pain and uncertainty for all involved. The implications of the Department of Health's (1998) *Caring for Children Away from Home: Messages for research* are clear: it is only in a tiny proportion (perhaps one in 60) of cases and thus probably in the most extreme situations that children will spend any time in residential care. The demands that this disarray and despair in families may cause for the children are nevertheless huge, meaning that many of the children who come into residential care do so in a whirlwind of distress and anxiety, and with a lasting legacy of emotional pain. These circumstances may help to account for the very high levels of apparent psychological disorder described earlier in Milligan's (2002) overview.

Every time a new child moves into a residential home, the impact of these strong emotions on the whole child care system – current residents, incoming resident, parents, staff, managers, and councillors – is considerable. In 1968 Stevenson wrote a paper entitled 'Reception into care – its meaning for all concerned' to capture this: ' ... there is a need to try and get inside the meaning of this experience ...'.

Noting the suffering that is likely to precede a move into a home, she wrote:

> All this makes the theme of reception into care sound sad, even depressing. But only by recognizing the truth about this infinitely complicated process can we begin to lay the foundations for good work. ... we need to look for the truth and depth of this experience for everyone involved in it. This demands courage and honesty from the professional workers. But it also offers a constructive and positive approach to an action which might otherwise seem destructive and negative. (p.17)
>
> (Quoted in Clough 2000, pp. 94–5)

One consistent finding of the research is of the huge and disruptive impact on settled groups of children in long-stay homes of emergency and short-term admissions of the most troubled children. One of the most urgent dilemmas facing local authorities is that of how to provide both suitable emergency accommodation, and medium to long-term care for those children who need it.

The use of residential care in two Welsh local authorities

It has already been noted that the number of looked after children placed in residential care has fallen over the past 30 years and is now quite small.

At this point we pause to look at the use that is made of residential homes, drawing for evidence on two studies by the Dartington social research unit of looked after children in two Welsh local authorities, one urban and one rural. Children who were living in residential care or had been placed there at any time were identified. Both samples were snapshot studies of children looked after at any one time, whose stays had exceeded three months. (This sample will emphasise the characteristics of long-stay cases and older children at the expense of younger children who leave accommodation quickly.)

In the city, a random sample of 100 children produced satisfactory data on 95 of them. On the day of the study, six were in residential care and another six had been placed therein at some point.

The six young people (two girls and four boys) living in residential care were aged between 13 and 16, and had all been over the age of 11 on entry to care. The other six (again two girls and four boys) who had been so placed in the past were also teenagers aged 13–16, but some had been younger on entry to care, two of them under five years of age and two between six and 11.

In the county area a similar pattern prevailed, although more use was made of residential care. In a sample of 88, nine were currently in residential placements and another eight had been so placed in the past. Of the nine in residential placements, four were aged between 11 and 15 and the other four were aged 16. On admission to care, eight of the nine were aged over nine. Of the other eight who had been in residential care, two were admitted to care under the age of four and the rest as teenagers.

This evidence confirms that most looked after children are not in residential care. The studies reveal a figure of around 8 per cent for these long-stay children. However, another 8 per cent will have been placed residentially at some point. All of the young people currently in residence are of secondary school age; half of them are aged 16. The majority were also first looked after over the age of 11, but a third (31 per cent) of those who have ever been so placed will have been first looked after under the age of 11, and 14 per cent under the age of five.

If these figures from the Dartington studies are reworked for those children aged 10 or more, we find that the figures for the city rise to 14 per cent currently in residence and 14 per cent at any one time. The figures for the county are 23 per cent currently and 44 per cent at any one time.

When the needs of the children are scrutinised, it is clear that the main reason for choosing residential care is to control or improve difficult behaviour, and that the other functions suggested by Beedell and Berridge, such as aiding admissions or keeping siblings together, no longer seem to apply. Lack of control and behaviour that is difficult to manage are the two overwhelming predictive factors for a residential placement, showing a multiplier effect of 12 over those without behaviour problems. These difficulties are manifest in several areas, such as the relatively high incidence of poor relationships with peers, suspicion of professionals and statements of special educational needs. But the relationship is less strong in the opposite direction.

While it is the case that most young people placed residentially display behaviour problems, only a minority of all the young people with such problems are in residential care. Of the 35 young people with behaviour problems in the city sample, only 10 are or have been in residential care. Similarly, these placements apply to only two young people without behaviour problems. Thus, 25 of the 35 young people displaying needs associated with behaviour problems have never been placed residentially.

One or two children entering residential care in the past might have been admitted in an emergency, but the overwhelming reason for staying is associated with the child's behaviour. For current placements, this comprises adolescent acting out, in one or two cases requiring specialist therapy; for placement at any time, it can include different behaviours associated with trauma and abuse, such as self-harm or extreme withdrawal.

Compared with other looked after children, the harm inflicted by parents on these children is less of an issue, and when it does occur it tends to be emotional rather than physical. Levels of neglect are also lower, and in a third of cases it was the parents who approached children's services for help. However, there are some important family characteristics: 70 per cent of the young people come from single-parent families and 20 per cent have parents with a chronic mental health problem.

The benefits of residential placements

Traditionally, residential care has been seen as offering several benefits. These are to provide stability and a stimulating environment, to widen cultural and educational horizons, to create a framework for emotionally secure relationships with adults and to provide a setting for intensive therapeutic work. These have to be set against difficulties of providing unconditional love, constraints on children's emotional development, poor staff continuity and marginalisation of children's families and other welfare services.

Of all the researchers considered, Whitaker and colleagues are the most optimistic about residential care. They conclude that, although there is no list of circumstances under which residential care should be a preferred option, there are occasions when residential care could be helpful:

- when there was a deficit in attachment-forming capacity and a young person could benefit from having available a range of carers
- when a young person had a history of having abused other children
- when a young person felt threatened by the prospect of living in a family or needed respite from it
- when multiple potential adult attachment figures might forestall a young person from emotionally abandoning his or her own parents
- when the emotional load of caring for a very disturbed or chaotic young person was best distributed among a number of carers
- when the young person preferred residential care to any form of family care, and would sabotage family care if it was provided.

CRITICISMS OF RESIDENTIAL CARE

In a recent review of research into residential and foster care, Rushton (2002) is less convinced of the merits of residential care than are Whitaker and colleagues. He expresses concern that staff in residential homes have no training or contact with Child and Adolescent Mental Health Services (CAMHS) to help them deal with the problems they face. He suggests, as do Sinclair and colleagues, that all of the treatments offered to troubled and troublesome teenagers can be delivered in foster care where there is less likelihood of bullying, sexual harassment and delinquent cultures. In contrast to Whitaker, he argues that when children have attachment difficulties, therapeutic foster care seems preferable. But given the control difficulties that some young people present, there is probably a need for a small number of high-quality residential establishments for children who cannot be accommodated any other way, or for whom there is a policy to keep them out of prison.

The use of residential services is also influenced by the views that are held about the quality of provision. There has been widespread recognition that many children looked after by local authorities have not been as well served as they should. Some children have found the services provided by the state offer them the chance to develop in new ways; others have found that the very services designed to 'look after' them have failed to provide well enough for their care and development; at the worst some have suffered serious abuse.

RECTIFYING THE WEAKNESSES OF RESIDENTIAL CARE

Statements of principle

There has been a significant attempt by the UK government and the National Assembly for Wales to rectify the problems just discussed. One approach considers all children and young people, viewing children looked after by local authorities as part of the wider group, in effect as young citizens; a second examines the failings of systems and reports on how to rectify them; a third sets out good practice guidance. Many documents start with the rights of children as services are provided in the context of policy frameworks and guidance. Thus the *Response to Lost in Care* (National Assembly for Wales 2000e, p.8) includes the following statement:

> The National Assembly for Wales endorses the key principles of the rights of children defined in the United Nations Convention on the Rights of the Child as being at the heart of the strategic approach.
> - Participation – children are active citizens in the world and have rights to their own opinions to express them and have them fully taken into account;
> - Protection – children are vulnerable and have the right to be protected in various ways;
> - Provision – children have rights to proper standards of physical care, education and health.

At the same time, the *Children First Programme* was initiated in Wales in 1999. The programme's original objectives were:

- to ensure that children in need and children looked after gain maximum life chance benefits from education opportunities, healthcare and social care;

- to ensure that children are protected from emotional, physical and sexual abuse and neglect
- to ensure that children are securely attached to carers capable of providing safe and effective care
- to ensure that young people leaving care, as they enter adulthood, are not isolated and are able to participate socially and economically as citizens
- to ensure that children with specific social needs arising out of disability or a health condition are living in families or other appropriate settings in the community where their assessed needs are adequately met and reviewed
- to ensure that referral and assessment procedures discriminate between different types and levels of need and produce a timely and effective service response
- to ensure that resources are planned and provided at levels which represent best value for money, allow for choice and different responses for different needs and circumstances (Welsh Office Circular 20/99).

In 2003–4 further objectives were added:

- to actively involve users and carers in planning implementation and review of services
- to ensure that local authorities have effective complaints procedures and promote access to advocacy for children
- to ensure that social care workers and foster carers are appropriately skilled, trained and qualified and to promote the uptake of training at all levels.

Assessments by the Social Services Inspectorate, Wales (SSIW)

Information about the performance of residential centres comes in part from the bodies responsible for regulation and inspection. Following the revelation of abuse within residential establishments for children, the SSIW conducted inspections of residential child care services run by social services departments (SSDs). It is important to note that the inspections were carried out between 1996 and 1997, when the authorities were newly established. Further, there will have been significant changes in structure and practice. Nevertheless it is useful to examine the findings so that we can ask whether or not they are 'true for us today'. Some of the areas focused on in the inspections, such as clarity of purpose for the establishment, are similar to those shown to be important in the research review above.

Children's services plans: All local authorities were required to produce plans which, in relation to residential homes, should ensure that, 'The function of the home makes a planned and explicit contribution to an integrated range of services for children within a defined geographic area' (SSIW standard, A1). Inspectors noted specific problems with some of the plans:

■ They failed to show ways in which residential homes were integrated into the wider child care system.
■ They depicted residential homes as 'last resort' rather than having positive benefit.
■ They did not clarify the role of specific homes and their relationship to other homes, Thus some had been renamed 'children's centres' without any comment on the significance of the change of name.
■ Structures were not developed to help homes achieve their designated function.
■ There was no strategy to reduce unplanned admissions.
■ They spoke about necessary cooperation between social services, education and health without specifying whether there had been agreements to ensure the contributions to be made by departments.

Some of these points touch on what we would term the enduring dilemmas for residences for children. What is their function? How do they fit into a wider system? How can their function be protected from emergencies?

Planning for children: The reports note good and bad planning. In the poor plans:

■ The reason (or problem) why someone moved into a home was defined as a need.
■ There was minimal assessment of a child's needs.
■ Needs were described generally, as were actions to follow. There was lack of specificity, of targets and of timescales for action.
■ Children were minimally involved. Even when more fully involved, they might not see the plan as useful for them.
■ There was minimal involvement from health and education.

Relationships between staff and children: Given the recognised importance of relationships for children's developments, it is heartening to find that in all the reports relationships were seen as good. In different places they are described as warm and trusting, with staff being described as sensitive and responsive, having genuine concern; children thought staff were 'committed'. Dealing with very difficult to manage child behaviour led sometimes to greater distance between staff and children. Staff were thought to need more support in this area from external managers.

Relationships between staff and other professionals: There were good relationships between field and residential social workers, but frequently these relationships were characterised by tensions, with field social work staff changing rapidly and failing to report back on outcomes of events such as child protection enquiries.

External management: This varied from the exceptional (with an external manager playing a significant role in ensuring that a home could survive through a time of crisis, getting to know staff and children very well) to poor in places where managers (and councillors) either did not know or failed to fulfil their responsibilities in relation to monitoring of the homes. Nor did they provide good enough support for staff.

Life style: Children were wearing clothes that were thought to be appropriate; most had sufficient privacy, with single rooms (though sometimes only because of under-occupancy), and usually locks on the doors. Food presented different sorts of problems. It is clear from comments that SSIW inspectors thought that one communal meal a day was valuable. At one home the notion of choice for the children meant that they got what they wanted, when they wanted, with little regard for diet or sharing of the event. Staff said that they were anxious to avoid institutionalising the children. Some homes bought via bulk purchasing, again a practice that was criticised by SSIW staff. The reason for the criticism seems based on the idea that children should learn about buying food. However, buying locally does not ensure this, and does demand that staff spend time in shopping. Our point is that there are dilemmas in providing services.

Records: Some were good, conveying pictures of children as individuals, being seen as useful by children and setting clear and specific objec- tives. It should be noted that many homes had no administrative support. Nevertheless it is important to note that the value of records did not seem to have been understood: their part in helping to focus thinking on planning for a child, and their ability to aid monitoring, both in relation to children but also activities within the home. Many agencies did not have good enough review systems so that it was common for reviews of some children not to be held on time, sanctions and absence books not to be kept up to date and inspection reports not to be acted upon. It was not common for children to see files as valuable for them: to look at; to write in, setting out their views; to provide a record for children of their lives; and to record current planning objectives on their behalf.

Staffing: Comparatively few staff were professionally qualified and many had had little training. Staff shortages were common, and this meant that frequently it was not possible for staff to attend training courses. Surprisingly, staff were more settled than might have been predicted, with many homes having a considerable proportion of experienced staff; SSIW inspectors noted the skills of staff in managing difficult situations.

Changing function: Many homes were running with small numbers, sometimes because of greater use of fostering, sometimes because of cessation of admissions following problems in managing children's behaviour, sometimes because of changing ideas of the functions of children's homes. At the same time some authorities were trying to bring back children from out of authority placements. There is virtually no discussion of the very high costs of running residential establishments with very small numbers of children, especially alongside demands that there should be working night staff in each home.

The local authority as corporate parent: It is apparent that, in many places, the nature of the responsibility of councillors for the well-being of children looked after by the authority had not been understood or acted on. However there were other problems of corporate parenting, in particular related to education. The well-being of looked after children does not rest solely with the social services department: recognition by education authorities of their responsibility is minimal, and there is virtually no record of agreements between education and social services departments about education. The picture is one of some good individual work (between staff in homes and schools, or between home and school) but of hardly any interdepartmental drive to ensure standards. There were some statements of the importance of cooperation.

Health authorities: Relationships with health staff seemed better but, in part, this may be because the demands on the system were not so great. Nevertheless there were frequent references to good partnership between health and social services, though, with one exception, there was inadequate access to the CAMHS.

Joint reviews of children and family services

Joint reviews, carried out by teams from the Audit Commission, SSIW and the National Assembly for Wales examine 'how well the public is being served by services locally'. We read the five reports undertaken in 2001 and 2002, together with an overview document looking at the outcome of reviews from 1999 and 2000, and summarise the findings below.

The main conclusions from these reports about children's services are set out below:

Collaboration and partnership: There was evidence of good collaborative work between departments and agencies in *producing* plans but that there had to be more focus on delivering them.

Variations in quality within services: The quality of services for vulnerable children is variable: one authority 'has developed many high quality services for vulnerable children'; there was one example of 14 separate referrals for one child in 29 months, with each being treated as a separate event.

Management structures: A 'corporate parenting' approach from councillors was thought essential; management structures had significant impact on management of services.

Assessment: Assessments were sometimes completed too quickly; a holistic rather than task focused assessment was needed.

Monitoring and reviews: Again, there was evidence of varied performance with children's services often reported as underdeveloped.

Field social workers and staffing: There were frequent interruptions in social work support in many places, which contrasted with a welcoming town centre office and all children having an allocated social worker. One authority had had 60 per cent staff turnover in children's teams since 1998–9. Too often authorities had to rely on newly qualified staff.

Services for children with disabilities: Reports echoed known variations across agencies in quality of assessments and services for disabled children; length of wait for respite care; services, including inter-agency cooperation for children with complex needs; planning for children transferring to adult services.

Emergency or unplanned placements: Some authorities made frequent use of emergency placements, and many needed to improve access outside office hours for mental health service users and foster carers.

Children's homes: One home designed 'to meet the needs of five young people with particularly complex needs, and to prepare them for a more permanent placement' did not have adequate operational and management systems in place before opening, nor was there a key worker system in place. Homes were regularly over number and outside statement of purpose. Homes were affected by turnover, staff sickness and heavy use of pool staff; ability to provide stable care was affected though staff groups remain committed.

Leaving care: Leaving care teams were rated highly by young people. If young people left care before 18, bed and breakfast might be the only option. Better links with housing would improve provision, especially as housing authorities might not let directly to anyone under 18.

Services for people from ethnic minorities: Despite the relatively high proportion of the population with a minority ethnic background, there is a poor understanding of the needs of these service users by staff.

Services for children with mental health needs: There were frequent reports of services under-resourced and fragmented as well as hard to access. An integrated service for assessment and therapeutic intervention was needed. A shortage of Welsh-speaking psychiatrists was noted and, as with services for disabled young people, the transition from adolescent to adult service caused problems.

Planning and placements: Many authorities had rising numbers of looked after children and struggled to cope. In one authority it was noted that the service to looked after children would be improved with additional resources to support return home within first six weeks; better matching of the child's need to placement and better support to foster parents; and clarifying purpose and occupancy level of each residential home. The high number of out-of-county placements in some authorities was also recorded. In another authority there was a gap in accessing therapeutic support for troubled children and a need to concentrate on rehabilitation and permanency planning for children already in the system.

Spending: The costs of social services and of children's services within social services differed significantly between authorities. One authority committed the same level of resources to funding 14 out-of-county placements as it committed to the remainder of care placements.

Educational provision for looked after children in Wales

In 2001 SSIW and Her Majesty's Inspectorate for Education and Training in Wales (Estyn) reported on inspections in four contrasting local authorities during 1999–2000 of education services for looked after children. In contrast to the information in the section above, this report covers both children being fostered and those in residential homes. The key findings are:

- Most children are in full-time education and making satisfactory progress.
- A minority are not receiving full-time education. Usually these are the ones with greatest need. They are under-achieving; they are further disadvantaged by delays in completing assessments and arranging educational placements.
- Local authorities have positive intentions to work corporately but responsibility for the children's education is often unclear. Implementation of policies is slow as is monitoring their effectiveness.
- LEAs and SSDs do not have compatible information systems.
- Children, parents, carers and schools are working more closely together.
- SSD reviews are held on time but do not give enough attention to education.
- Workers appreciate the need to listen to and involve children in consultation and decision-making. In practice they do not find it easy to balance children's wishes with their needs, and their rights and responsibilities.

Some problems endured from earlier reports. There was uncertainty over how to deliver education for the children who were most troublesome or most rejecting of education. Even when education and social services staff began to understand each other's systems and priorities there were difficulties in integrating systems. Staff shortages in social services management reduced the ability of departments to plan and monitor. There was potential to learn from what works successfully, and there was a dawning recognition in official documents that consulting with children and talking about 'choice' does not necessarily lead to solid negotiation amongst all parties as to the best educational opportunities and solutions for children.

Summary of the significant problems in provision identified in inspection and audit reports

The points made by the inspection and audit reports discussed above can be summarised as follows:

- There was evidence of good collaborative work between departments and agencies in *producing* plans but there needed to be more focus on delivering them.
- The quality of services for vulnerable children is variable between and within authorities.
- A 'corporate parenting' approach from councillors was thought essential. This should involve social services, education and housing authorities, the latter being of particular importance when children were leaving care. Management structures had significant impact on management of services.
- Assessments were sometimes completed too quickly; a holistic rather than task-focused assessment was needed.
- There were frequent interruptions in social work support.
- Reports echoed known variations in agencies on: quality of assessments and services for disabled children; length of wait for respite care; services, including inter-agency cooperation for children with complex needs; planning for children transferring to adult services.
- Some authorities made frequent use of emergency placements, and many needed to improve access outside office hours for mental health service users and foster carers.
- Despite the relatively high proportion of the population with a minority ethnic background, there is a poor understanding of the needs of these service users by staff.
- Services for children with mental health needs were reported to be under-resourced and fragmented as well as hard to access.

■ Many authorities had rising numbers of looked after children and struggled to cope.

PLANNING FROM EVIDENCE

The research base

The evidence, discussed earlier, shows the factors that influence the quality of residential life for children. In particular, weight should be given to:

■ leadership of a home
■ congruity of objectives between staff in the home, the home manager, external management and wider social systems
■ establishments of appropriate cultures within the homes.

Key influences on practice were:

■ rate of turnover of the young people
■ proportion of emergency placements
■ mix of young people
■ number of young people not in school
■ stability of membership in the staff group
■ composition of both young people and staff with respect to ethnicity and gender
■ feelings of security among staff within their own organisation
■ presence or absence of conflict with managers
■ level of morale.

However, there are a number of areas where the research evidence is either not conclusive or fails to back conventional wisdom. Four such areas will be further examined.

AREAS OF UNCERTAINTY

Staff training and professional qualifications

Nearly every report on residential care bemoans the low numbers of qualified staff. Indeed, on the day we were drafting this section of the report, Des Browne, then minister responsible for Health, Social

Services and Public Safety in Northern Ireland, reported on a 'Search for excellence in children's services':

> We are still the only region to have a policy intention of achieving a fully social work qualified residential child care staff; today we have 60 per cent of residential workers qualified compared, with some 5 per cent in England.
> *(Media release, 13 June 2003)*

In an earlier section we looked at whether there was evidence that qualified staff improved outcomes for children. We cannot find such evidence. However, we argued that *appropriate qualification* is important. We think it is likely to have three significant results. The first is that staff will have a better basis for understanding children and practice. Second, staff will have more of a common framework for their practice, which should enhance a key objective of shared values and approaches. Third, it is likely to enhance their status and to lead to higher-quality recruits into the profession.

Our suggestion is that the National Assembly takes time to review the impact of training patterns in other countries of the United Kingdom as well as the potential of the social pedagogy model. Northern Ireland has significantly higher levels of qualified staff: but has this led to improvements in the services? Scotland has developed a specialist centre for residential child care: again, what has been the impact?

There are attractions in the creation of a specialist centre in that this becomes a place for the development of knowledge about good practice. As such it should become a support for staff. So, on initial review, this idea seems worth pursuing. Such a centre might be able to consider ways of incorporating theory and research evidence in practice. For example, what are the best ways to operationalise Brown and colleagues' linear model in which the structure of the home determines the staff culture, and the staff culture determines the child culture, which in turn, determines outcome for homes and for children?

However, we also think it essential and urgent that there is a review of the best means of training (as opposed to assessing) care staff and managers. We do not think that the new degree in social work offers effective training for managers. Training must take account of, and focus upon, the realities of residential life. When points like this are made, some people stress the fact that much of residential living is concerned with the practicalities of everyday life, so that staff need such skills. We endorse that, but think it essential that there is at the heart an understanding that staff are working alongside children who have faced considerable disturbance. About half have diagnosable mental health problems. Staff need a capacity to understand and respond to children's pain.

Staff numbers

If analogies were to be taken from schooling, it would be assumed that more staff would lead to better practice. Again the research evidence challenges what can be seen as a 'taken for granted assumption'. A higher staff–child ratio has not been shown to produce better outcomes. We think that there is an inter-relationship that has not been understood between:

- the size of the establishment
- the quality of staff
- staffing systems
- the understanding or use of the group of children.

As long ago as 1975 Millham, Bullock and Cherett argued that leaving children free to do as they wanted in their out of school time, under a guise of liberalism, was failing to intervene in the children's world. The recent work of Brown and colleagues (1998) elaborates and amends that position. We suggest that the evidence on staff numbers has to be seen in the context of the way in which staff are working with the group of children.

Choice

Perhaps more controversially, given the overarching framework of the project we have been asked to undertake, we have found no evidence that links greater choice to improved outcomes. However, it is clear that, in a consumerist world, children state that they want more choice, and that social work staff involved in placement repeatedly highlight the problems posed for them in having too few choices. The one area where the evidence does link lack of choice to worse outcomes is in foster care, where the shortage of foster homes has a direct consequence of children having to wait longer for a permanent placement. Our suggestion is that slogans such as 'Choice protects' should be unpicked.

There is an assumption in the wider health and social care fields that if there are enough places, people will select the better establishments and the worse will go out of business. Given the small numbers in residential care for children and the very great difficulty for any child trying to initiate a move, that argument does not appear to have relevance. The much more important question is that of deciding the framework for service provision:

- What types of places are wanted?
- What are their functions?
- Where are they to be placed?

Indeed, it is necessary to consider who is expected to have greater choice: child, family or placing agency?

Two particular aspects emerge from research as critical in planning:

1. Local/general or specialist/regional resources.
2. Managing emergency/short-term placements and stability within individual residential establishments.

With regard to the first point, guidance concerning placements over the last 20 years has stressed the advantages of keeping children near to home. The original reason for this was to ensure that links with family were maintained. More recently the maintenance of friendships and continued use of local facilities have been stressed. However there are competing arguments:

- Perhaps more important than physical distance to the maintenance of links with families is the style of the residence in terms of its welcome, inclusion of families and encouragement to visit, and the emotional distance or otherwise with which families are treated.
- Some children should be placed away from their links with people in the local communities, and on occasion, away from being too close to families.
- Some children would benefit from more specialist resources, in particular when they offer a therapeutic perspective or the development of skills.

This is an important topic in Wales, given the numbers of children who are placed out of their own authority and, indeed, the numbers who are placed across the border in England. Placements in England are used in particular for specialist resources. There is also the problem of numbers of children placed by English authorities in Wales.

With regard to the second point mentioned above, the debate concerning small and local versus larger and more specialist resource is linked to that of how to manage short-term resources. There are numerous strands.

The first is that some children currently living at home would be better served by planning that considered the sort of residential home that would be appropriate if there were to be a breakdown in arrangements. This would lead to fewer emergency placements.

The second is that there is substantial evidence from SSIW and other reports, as well as accounts from field social work and residential staff, that many children are placed temporarily or for longer periods in placements that are inappropriate because there are no short-term facilities available. The other side of this coin is the frequent immense disruption to establishments caused by movement in one or more emergency placements.

A third aspect is the fear that has always existed about short-term facilities, such as reception centres of old, that they would lead to additional moves for children, would result in placements being made without enough thought because there were places where children could be 'held'; and that they in turn would become full and be unable to find places to which the children should move.

Size of residential home

When the size of residential homes is considered, the conventional wisdom that 'small is beautiful' is backed by some research evidence. Sinclair and Gibbs (1998) are categoric that smaller homes performed better. Chipenda-Dansokho and colleagues (2003), however, argue that size has to be understood in the wider context of aims and structures of the organisation. We think that this is an important area for the National Assembly for Wales to determine its policy.

The case for small homes would seem to be based on the greater potential for individualising experiences for children, the potential for the home to merge more easily in the local community, the greater opportunity for staff to have oversight of what is going on with the accompanying benefit of reducing the likelihood of bullying by other children.

Those arguing for larger homes would cite: the high costs of small homes; the greater likelihood of one child disrupting the whole life of the place; the potential to work positively with the group of children; and the opportunity to develop specialist resources.

Our own view is that size of home is one factor to be considered alongside many others. In general, there do seem to be advantages in smaller homes, but this does not mean that getting smaller and smaller is getting better and better, nor that there is no place for what might be termed larger units as more specialist resources.

A SUMMARY OF THE RESEARCH MESSAGES ON RESIDENTIAL CARE FOR CHILDREN

Research does produce evidence of the characteristics of good residential homes and the structures that are needed to establish them. However, research evidence does not write a policy: the evidence has to be interpreted and judgements have to be made.

Many studies identify the components of good and effective practice. In doing this, they also reveal serious weaknesses in current services, such as failures to meet the mental health and educational needs of children. All stress the benefits of listening and responding to young people's views. In addition, managerial competence and the personal qualities of carers emerge as important factors, as does sensitivity to children's feelings of fear, loss and trauma. But a focus on process elements such as these has limitations, such as underplaying the fact that children go to school, mix with peers and have families to which they usually return, and polished management will only improve outcomes to a limited degree. Thus, much remains to be done in these areas.

There is also considerable evidence on the support, management and training that should underpin a professional service. Inadequate recruiting, supporting, retaining and training people for work with children are serious challenges, and managers face continual pressures of financial scrutiny and difficult decisions, such as the use of private and voluntary providers. Again, the research is clear about these problems and what needs to be done.

In terms of outcomes for children and families, however, the evidence is weaker. In many cases we simply do not know what to do for the best, and interventions can be an ad hoc mixture of experience, intuition, research, opportunism, obedience and pragmatism. The research seems to be more certain about what is harmful than what is enriching to children. Instability and poor attachments recur as factors likely to impair children's development but the discussion accompanying them is not always profound. Social work borrows concepts such as partnership, resilience and protective factors from other disciplines but applies them rather loosely to child care situations. Thus, many unknowns remain.

The reviews also highlight a gap between aspiration and reality, a feature that dogs many public services. How do we manage change and get the lofty recommendations of official reports implemented in the field? Delivery seems to be a perennial problem even when we are confident about what needs to be done. Again, there is little research on this process despite the likelihood of good intentions being thwarted at the final hurdle.

We do know, in contrast, more about the conditions necessary to fashion an effective children's service. We also know that each has a different time and resource implication and can only work in combination with others as part of a multifaceted reform strategy. No condition is sufficient on its own and weakness in one area will hinder progress in others. They include:

- knowledge about the needs of all disadvantaged children
- sound audit and assessment information and materials to gather and analyse it
- the need to take a holistic and longitudinal view of children and families
- the provision of a continuum of services
- clear perceptions of service avenues in response to different needs
- clear thresholds that allow children to follow different care careers
- a well managed and supported process
- (most important of all) the application of interventions that produce optimal outcomes for children and families.

BUILDING ON THE RESEARCH EVIDENCE

Getting residential care right: establishing objectives, systems and processes

It will always be difficult to get residential care right. The unpredictability of the work, the young people's troubled histories and the problems associated with communal living all complicate the work. Residential care relies on a set of congruities between the needs of children and residential regimes and between the seemingly opposing aims of control and welfare. While the changes recommended by researchers, inspectors and others will not guarantee success, the evidence is that good outcomes for both homes and children are more likely if these conditions apply than if they do not.

Residential homes are also powerful environments. Their effects on children's behaviour and thus on their welfare are considerable. By taking a broad view, needs, services and outcomes can be effectively related and the accountability that should accompany good management can be enforced.

Our intention in this section is to highlight areas for consideration concerning the future development of residential services for children in Wales. At this stage we are setting out the research evidence and highlighting *areas for consideration*; we are not putting forward plans for action. These will follow after the ideas have been discussed in different settings. Inevitably, any of the six questions below merge with other questions: responses to one are likely to influence those to another.

1. Which children will want – or be judged to need – a short or long stay in a residential home?

It is apparent from the research evidence already examined that the use of residential homes will vary with fashion, new understandings and resources. So in the end responses to this question must take account of the context of residential care in Wales. Yet it remains essential to start with examining the behaviour of children and asking, what would best help them? We have noted above from SSIW reports the frequency with which a problem is defined as a need. The main reason for choosing residential care in Wales has been to control or improve difficult behaviour. Is this satisfactory?

2. What sorts of services are wanted?

This question is complex because it can be examined in two ways: the first is to think about the types of residential provision that are judged valuable; the second is to think about the types of service that arise from children's needs, and then to consider whether or not these are best provided in residential homes or not. Included in this topic is the central question as to the ways in which residential services fit into the pattern of services for children in Wales.

Good planning for services demands that professionals should set out attainable outcomes in all aspects of a child's life by asking, for example:

▪ Where is a child likely to be living in two, five, 10 years time?
▪ What is the nature of family relationships likely to be?
▪ What is to be expected in terms of education, health and social
  relations?

Knowledge of aspects like this should enable thinking as to how residence and other services can contribute to good outcomes – as distinct from considering what outcomes can be salvaged from the residential context.

In earlier sections of this report we set out the classification systems used to describe the functions of different establishments. In brief, they had a focus on education at one end and a focus on serious psychological needs and behavioural problems at the other. Most residential child care establishments fall into the groupings that have several functions, even if priority is given to one. Thus a home might aim to work with children who have social, psychological and behavioural needs *and* to work with family members *and* to help children develop educational skills. The classification is helpful in demanding consideration of what is wanted from residential homes. Regulatory systems, properly demand that individual homes set out their purpose. Our point is that the National Assembly for Wales should consider the sorts of services that it wants residential homes to provide. Further it should consider the sorts of establishments in which those services should be provided.

Working with private and voluntary providers ought not to result in a placing local authority being dependent on the sorts of facilities and services that such providers choose to develop, albeit taking account of the viability of their establishments. This may leave authorities with a surplus of certain types of provision and underdevelopment of others. Thus local authorities, in conjunction with the National Assembly, should develop a strategic plan.

It is worth noting that a distinguishing feature in the classification was the extent to which parents were involved. It is important for the National Assembly to consider the sort of involvement that best supports the children and young people placed in residences.

3. What are the outcomes that are wanted from residential homes?

With this we are posing again the central question of what residential services are designed to achieve, though we are framing it in the context of outcomes. There has been much written about inputs, outputs and outcomes. Inputs are seen as the resources that are put in (for example, staff hours worked, the support from other children, buildings and facilities), outputs are the consequences of the input (such as meals cooked, a clean building and reports written), and the term 'outcomes' is intended to capture what has been achieved in a wider perspective. The input of an hour worked by a staff member may be an output of an hour's conversation with a child; defining the outcome will involve making a judgement on the value of that conversation.

Thus, at the most basic we are asking what it is that residential homes are expected to achieve. In answering the question it is essential that account is taken of what is known about what residential homes can achieve. There is abundant evidence that:

- children can enjoy living in good residential establishments
- children's behaviour can be significantly changed during their stay in residence
- children can gain skills in education or preparation for work *and* can tackle long standing health problems.

Some establishments, most noticeably those claiming to have a therapeutic perspective, aim to influence the way in which children will manage themselves and their lives after they leave the residence.

This question about outcomes is critical not only in that it demands consideration of what can reasonably be expected from residential facilities. It is also essential that the ways in which the performances of residential establishments are measured reflect both priorities and likely accomplishments.

4. What are the characteristics of good services?

We have set out in earlier sections different views of the characteristics of good services which take account of the perspectives of children, staff, researchers and the official perspectives from guidance and regulations. These should be examined to test whether they are seen as the appropriate characteristics for promotion by the National Assembly for Wales. Consideration should be given to whether some characteristics have greater importance than others.

5. What are the systems and processes that help to produce good services?

We have noted in different places that there is consistent and reliable evidence of the characteristics of good services and the types of structures that will help to create them. Thus, for example, it is safe to conclude that good residential care demands that there is agreement in different systems as to the goals for residential care. In this way children, parents, staff, line management, external management and the wider community will be in general agreement as to what residential centres are aiming to do. Yet it remains extremely difficult to establish systems that will produce what is wanted.

The local authority is a corporate parent: it has responsibility for the well-being of the child in different areas. Research and audit reports have produced evidence of the importance for children's education of partnership between education and social services departments. Guidance repeatedly demands that there are procedures in place to ensure such partnership. Yet the educational experiences of looked after children remain patchy. Individual schools and residences are dependent on their individual staff; each place operates within its own system and it is clear that performance targets for schools have influenced the willingness of head teachers and managers to take pupils who are thought to be 'hard to teach' and 'disruptive'. Neither writing platitudinous statements that there must be cooperation nor condemning residential and foster carers for failing to produce children with better educational achievements will ensure that children are enthused and supported in developing educational skills.

The question of how to achieve the desired outcomes can be seen in other areas. A good working relationship between adult and child is essential if the child is to have a worthwhile experience. From research we can specify the components of such relationships, for example treating children with respect or reliability. Yet we know comparatively little of how, consistently and in different places, to ensure that children have good working relationships.

6. What are the shared objectives and practice of partnerships?

The consequences of failures of separate departments is widely reported. It is necessary to repeat the calls for social services, health, education and housing authorities to work together and, indeed, to recognise their separate responsibilities for looked after children. Grand claims are made on behalf of the children that they have basic rights to be included in services and not to be further disadvantaged by the experience of being looked after by the local authority. There seems to be better cooperation and recognition of responsibilities in some authorities than others. Further understanding is needed of what leads to better practice.

DEVELOPING RESIDENTIAL SERVICES THAT MATCH THE WANTS AND NEEDS OF CHILDREN

We start by setting out background factors and objectives for planning:

- The importance of understanding the nature of the problems that children present.
- Planning of services ought to follow categorisation of children's needs, but is dependent on knowing the numbers of children with different sorts and patterns of needs so that appropriate services may be developed.
- There must be clarity about what the intervention on behalf of the state is designed to achieve.
- It is important to determine how objectives such as stability of placement or good leadership can be achieved.

- The children who move into residential homes and schools are likely to face pervasive problems that have not been easy to manage in other settings.
- Children in residential homes often feel that they are excluded and treated as abnormal.
- Residential provision has to be evaluated in the context of the total lives of children. Too often residential staff have been castigated for failing to remedy long-standing problems; their contribution has not been seen in this context.

Alongside the listing of objectives like these are statements of values and rights. Thus, as active citizens, the Welsh Assembly Government (WAG) asserts the right of children:

- to participate by stating their views and having them taken into account
- to proper standards of services
- to be protected.

However, although few would disagree with these, it is less clear how such rights are to be exercised. There are numerous similar questions about implementation: What does 'listening' mean? How is it to be decided whether their views have to be taken into account? What is a proper standard of service?

Neither statements of purpose nor assertions of the rights of children on their own lead to better practice. It is our view that the WAG should review these documents and compile a succinct summary of the key items that form the framework for the practice of residential child care in Wales. Energy must then go into the development of structures and systems for better practice.

In brief, asserting that children must have choice or be listened to provides little information as to what is to happen when there are competing choices: for instance, what is to be done when the choice is between a local home without specialist support and a more specialised home where the way of working and level of resourcing is thought by staff to meet better the needs of children? So without more elaboration, these discussions will remain undeveloped.

When children's lives go awry, the state should support the child and family with the best possible services, aiming to maintain and develop positive aspects in their lives and reduce those that are harmful. It is important to recognise that many children in Wales face such difficulties but do not enter care. Those that do enter care usually experience a breakdown in their family circumstances coupled with structural forces such as a run-down environment, unemployment, instability within their own families, poor educational opportunities and a lack of belief that the future holds much opportunity.

It is the wish of the Welsh Assembly to develop a comprehensive and integrated children's service that is needs-led, evidence-based and provides value for money. Given that aspiration, it is clear from the evidence discussed that a continuum of services for children in need has to be available, and that within this totality, provision for looked after children will be prominent. It is equally obvious that services are inter-related and change in one will affect others. Indeed, the terms 'fostering' and 'residential', although separate administratively, may no longer reflect the reality of what best meets children's needs. They are merely contexts for looking after children away from home, and much depends on what happens therein. Although there are differences with regard to such things as the ultimate responsibility of carers and the location of the provision, from the child's view a large foster family may not feel very different from a small residential home. Similarly, in the course of a care career, a young person may move between the two, several times in some cases.

Residential services must be planned in the context of all services for children in need. This requires an understanding of the background, experiences and presenting problems of all vulnerable children in a locality and the use of appropriate assessment materials to chart their needs and careers. Paperwork is often criticised for diverting professionals from work with users. Therefore it is imperative that the information that is collected is appropriate and purposeful.

Local authorities should be in a position to differentiate between the individual children for whom they are responsible, considering their needs and planning appropriately. Assessment is the key to this. However good the framework, undertaking an assessment does not ensure that the assessment material is used to look at the services that are appropriate for that child. Too frequently, rather than looking at the needs of a child, staff will try various options in sequence, starting with less specialist foster care. If this fails, then a series of moves are likely through different types of foster care before different types of residential care are tried. We argue that assessment should be used to plan for a child, which might lead to some children being placed, appropriately, in a residential home at an earlier stage.

We raise parallel questions about the use that is made of records. Information collected should be accumulated to provide details of the ways that resources are used. There is no point in demanding time-consuming records if they are not used for review and planning: sound policies require reliable information and accurate auditing.

It is equally clear that foster and residential care are not monoliths and there is much variety within each category. It goes without saying that if services are to be matched to children's needs, many different types of foster and residential provision are required. The aim must be to help a particular child and family through practice validated as effective by research and delivered in a way that respects their individual circumstances and wishes.

PLANNING CHILDREN'S SERVICES IN WALES

'Children's services' are defined in the Green Paper for England and Wales, *Every Child Matters*, as services organised, not necessarily delivered, by health, education, social care and police and youth justice agencies with the intention of meeting a social need. They are focused on meeting children's needs by preventing and intervening to reduce impairment to development. Thus, any proposals for service development should avoid adopting the perspective of a hierarchy of services in which one set of provisions is designed to prevent the use of another. There will inevitably be a tendency for this to happen, but there is no point in setting up sophisticated residential services and then introducing another set of services to keep people out. In a needs-based system, the children directed to residential establishments would be those whose needs are best met by the experience.

Modifications to children's services are not brought about by single actions. A concerted strategy to reduce numbers of looked after children or to change the quality of their experience has to tackle admissions, lengths of stay, service quality and design and leaving processes. No one of these is sufficient on its own and any short-term gains they produce are unlikely to be maintained.

This policy perspective helps construct a needs-led and evidence-based approach to children's problems. It also encourages features of the modern child care service envisaged in the Green Paper, namely finding mechanisms to prioritise risk, setting out eligibility for services, ensuring that provision matches the needs of the child and identifying a single process leading to a continuum of interventions. Hopefully, this will also lead to perennial issues being addressed in more critical ways, such as by using family group conferences to avoid court proceedings.

It may help if this approach is illustrated diagrammatically. This will be done by beginning with all children in need, using the Children Act 1989 definition of impairment to health and development if no services are provided, and following through their possible service experiences. Two diagrams are needed, one showing the numbers in each situation *at any one time*, that is, a snapshot (Figure 3.1) and the other showing the numbers moving through the process *over the period of one year*, that is, a movie perspective (Figure 3.2). Each will give a different picture. Some figures, such as the number of looked after children, will be accurate, others fairly so, while some, such as those in need but unknown to children's services, will be unknown. It should be noted that the figures included are those that were available to the research team at the end of 2003.

Once this diagram has been constructed as fully as possible, at each stage in the process thresholds can be set to explain why children would be expected to proceed in different ways (see p. 102).

Differentiating between needs of young people

It is our view that the system of provision for children looked after in Wales should include a range of provision, clearly differentiated according to the levels and types of need amongst the different groups of children in varying circumstances, while allowing for the fact that there may be some overlap and movement between these groups.

Just as foster care is frequently differentiated into 'ordinary' or mainstream care and 'specialist' or 'treatment/therapeutic' oriented care, similar distinctions may need to be made in the provision of residential care.

The question of geographic spread will also come into the calculations here, as the variable size and populations of the Welsh local authorities

Figure 3.1 Services for children in need:
a snapshot view of children on any one day

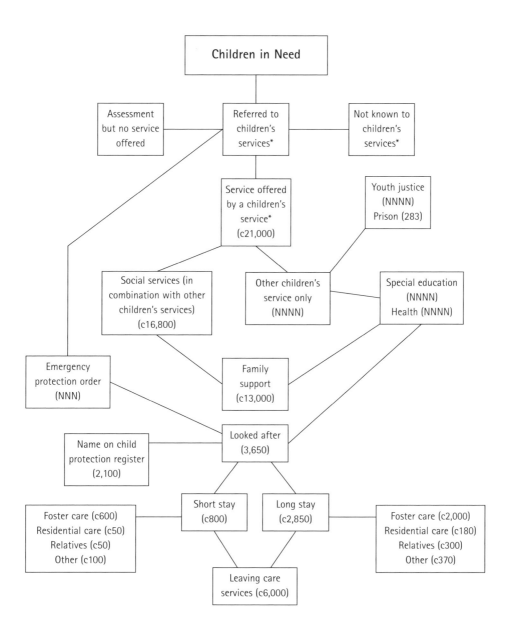

* 'Children's services' are defined as services organised not necessarily delivered by health, education, social care, police and youth justice agencies with the intention of meeting a social need.

Figure 3.2 Services for children in need: movie view of children in the process over the period of a year

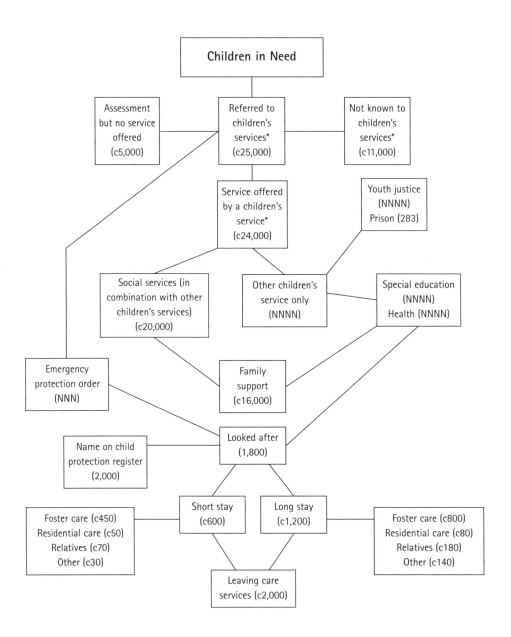

* 'Children's services' are defined as services organised not necessarily delivered by health, education, social care, police and youth justice agencies with the intention of meeting a social need.

mean that they do not each have the demography to support a viable residential provision. There may therefore need to be some sharing of resources and pooling of services, across local authority boundaries and in some cases across the whole country.

The range of needs to be met

In order to plan for the range of circumstances which will have to be addressed, some distinction will need to be made about the varying levels of emotional and psychological need of the young people entering the care system. While acknowledging that the categories set out below represent broad generalisations which will not fit the subtle nuances of individual cases, we are proposing a broad distinction between three groups of young people, as follows:

1. Children with relatively simple or straightforward needs

They will require either short-term or relatively 'ordinary' substitute care. These may be children from families that are comparatively stable and supportive, but in which there has been a crisis or difficulty around one or more family members' behaviour, needs or circumstances. There can be a reasonable expectation that after a period of substitute care the child will return to the family and/or progress towards adult life without being at serious risk of further harm.

These children's needs for care and support may be urgent (for example, following sudden family arguments or bereavement) but not necessarily drastic or long-term. Their psychological and emotional development may be at risk of some disruption but not to the extent of their needing 'treatment'. In most cases these children will go into foster care, although the evidence suggests that where they are offered a real choice, some of them will prefer to go into residential care, which may, for example, be perceived as offering less threat to or competition with their own family. They will usually benefit from staying in their existing schooling and with their current peer group; flexible, non-stigmatising and local care resources are most likely to be appropriate.

2. Children or families with deep-rooted, complex or chronic needs

These may be families in which there has been a long history of difficulty and disruption, including violence, abuse or neglect, or in which there may have been multiple episodes of substitute care. For some of these children the main evidence of their distress and emotional instability may be their unsafe, self-harming or unpredictable behaviour, but although this behaviour will need to be managed in order to stabilise their lives, the mere control of behaviour will not necessarily lead to any resolution of the underlying causes of this behaviour which more often than not lie in family histories and relationships.

Children in these circumstances are likely to require more than simply a substitute family, and will require more specialist care and other services, offering emotional and psychological support and treatment. Again these services may be provided in either foster or residential settings, and where possible and appropriate the child should be offered some choice. Such care will also need to provide a setting in which to coordinate and manage specialist work by others. Thus social work needs to be undertaken with families, with different services for different relatives so that any strength in family structures and relationships can be maintained.

3. Children with extensive, complex and enduring needs compounded by very difficult behaviour

Usually such behaviour is of a chronic nature originating much earlier in their childhood, often in the traumas of serious physical or sexual abuse. Their disturbance will often find expression in extremes of physical or sexual violence either within the family and/or at school or in their neighbourhood. This is behaviour that will often have led them into the juvenile justice system, or in some cases into the mental health system if it is viewed in these terms.

These children are likely to require more specialised and intensive resources such as a therapeutic community, an adolescent mental health unit, a small 'intensive care' residential setting or a secure unit. They can only be placed successfully in foster care if exceptionally high levels of extra support can be built in.

The routes by which these children currently arrive in placement are often haphazard, depending upon local knowledge of services and local beliefs and ideologies as well as upon local funding possibilities – and sometimes according to mere chance and luck. The level of need in such young people is great, and without successful intervention at this stage they are most likely to spend large proportions of their adult lives in prison, psychiatric services or homeless. We recommend that these children require considerable investment in specialist services, including high-quality residential care and aftercare, if they are to thrive, and if the risk of their incurring even greater long-term costs is to be reduced. These should focus on health, education, behaviour and family relationships, with the same proviso as in the second group, above.

THE NEED FOR EFFECTIVE AND EFFICIENT ASSESSMENT, INFORMATION AND PLANNING

The above categories are very broad, and are based upon generalised assumptions about children's social and emotional needs. In practice, however, such generalisations may be antithetical to individual children's welfare, and all decisions should be based upon careful observation and assessment of the needs of the child and its family. A way therefore needs to be found to enable children to receive a thorough and constructive assessment of their emotional and psychological need (as well as their educational, health and other needs), and for this assessment to be used as the basis of a positive plan for their care and treatment rather than as a (possibly unhelpful) label. The information should include those areas known to be significant for children's life trajectories and outcomes. We recommend that the WAG should investigate the adoption throughout the child welfare system of an agreed tool for the assessment of children's emotional needs and, equally important, ways of aggregating the information for management purposes. This would probably collect less (but certainly different) information than at present but do more with it. Arriving at a suitable assessment tool may require further developmental work, but those currently available 'off the shelf', such as the government's Assessment Framework and the Dartington practice tools *Paperwork* and *Aggregating Data on Children in Need*, offer a good starting point.

As we have already argued, following assessment, planning for children has to design services for today in the context of what is predicted about the future. It is only in this way that there will be the sort of planning, management and training that is needed to promote services that will help to achieve those aspirations.

If the looked after system is to be managed effectively in organisational and professional child care terms, there has to be a clear process that covers three parts of the service: entry, departure and those children who continue to be looked after, looking especially at their length of stay and predictions of their short and long-term outcomes. In combination, these three approaches should ensure that the right services are used for the right children for the right amount of time.

DEVELOPING A STRATEGY FOR WALES: THE ROLE OF RESIDENTIAL CARE IN CHILDREN'S SERVICES

It has become commonplace for reports such as this to stress that residential work must be valued in its own right as a specialist resource, and not seen as an unfortunate, possibly unwanted, fallback when all other options have failed. The title of the Wagner report in 1988, *A Positive Choice*, captured the hope. Repeating such statements takes us little further, though we endorse them wholeheartedly. Residential work will only be seen in this positive light when the activity and the staff from homes are recognised as skilled, purposeful and specialist in meeting the specific needs of children. Recognising residential care as a key part of a wider system will not on its own lead to greater value being placed on work within residential homes.

If residential care is to take a positive place in the continuum of services for looked after children, it is also important that thresholds are set and understood by the professionals involved. Thresholds are of two kinds. The first concerns the nature and severity of need necessary to require a service. The second concerns the response to that need, namely what professionals do to get the service they want – write a letter, send a social worker or call the police? Not all severe needs are met by residential care, and it may be used for relatively low level needs as part of an intervention. Thresholds are difficult to operate, but they are important to any effective system for two reasons. They ensure that the right children get the right service, and they promote consistent responses across different geographical areas, an important issue given the topography and population distribution of Wales.

Developing strategies at national, regional and local levels

Earlier we have argued for a national strategy based upon a planned response to assessed need. Here we consider further the development of these strategies. It is clear from our study of governmental reports together with comments made to us during this research that the placement of looked after children in Wales is driven more by a search for individual places for individual children than by an overview of the sorts of services that are needed, followed by plans to develop such services. We have examples of local authorities responding in very different ways:

- managing one or two residential homes themselves at levels one and two from our earlier descriptions
- contracting out such residential services to be provided by a voluntary or private organisation
- having no provision themselves, and looking to other local authorities or the private and voluntary sectors to provide all placements.

All authorities look outside their own organisation for the provision of the highly specialist services.

It would be useful for the WAG to commission work that would examine the use and costs to local authorities of getting services from different providers. We have no view that one agency is to be preferred to another. We think that the WAG and local authorities should better understand the costs and benefits of using different providers.

Another component is that the beliefs of individual workers or agencies influence placement. Some believe that no child should be placed in a residential home. Such divergence, akin to a hospital refusing certain well-accepted treatments, is not acceptable.

We have already set out the case for the WAG developing a national strategy in which residential care should be seen as a positive resource for the meeting of certain needs. In the context of that strategy we consider that each local authority should first determine its own needs and then determine the way to ensure the provision of appropriate services. Commissioning should take place in the context of a national and local plan. In doing this account should be taken of the distinctive characteristics of Welsh local authorities: the number of comparatively small authorities in terms of population and resources and the mix of sparse, rural areas and large conurbations. In addition, within the overall strategy, the WAG will have to develop the framework within which local authorities will make arrangements with other local authorities in their region.

We are not convinced that there are robust enough systems for the collection of information held by various parties on what works well in residential child care and what does not. For example the Care Standards Inspectorate for Wales (CSIW) as a regulatory body has the responsibility for reporting on individual homes. Yet staff may have views on good and less good developments. One possible improvement would be for these to be reported in a general way, perhaps akin to the reports of former children's inspectors. Russell, a Chief Inspector in the Home Office, commented in his 1914 report that parents should be involved in the disposal of their children, stating that that when English boys went to Welsh farms the farmer and his wife should be able to speak English! He seems to have aimed at encouraging staff to look at what they were doing:

> What would a Superintendent who insists on silence at meals think of
> the table manners of a member of the school staff who persisted in
> consuming his food in gloomy silence?
> *Home Office (1914)* Report of the Chief Inspector, *Cd. 8091*

Of course it is essential that the integrity and separateness of the CSIW not be compromised.

A structure for residential services

If the WAG strategy for residential child care were to be based upon planned response to assessed need, and there were a range of levels of service provided for the children in each of the broad groupings outlined above, one possible way of categorising these different levels of service is set out below.

Level one: mainstream

Each local authority should have, or have access to, at least one children's home. The task of these units will be to provide good quality daily care and support for children who need to live away from home, perhaps for a short period during a family crisis or following an episode of difficult behaviour, and who either do not wish to live in a family or are thought to be unsuited to foster care. These will largely be children in category one (above) with some from category two.

These units should be located close to the children's home town so that, as far as possible, they can remain within their existing peer group and educational facilities. There should be good liaison between the unit staff and the children's families, and careful professional liaison with staff from other disciplines such as health and education. Exit routes and strategies also need to be well established. It should be noted that, although such homes are sometimes referred to as 'ordinary children's homes', they still require *extra*ordinary levels of skill and knowledge from the staff, who are caring for children in the midst of considerable crisis and upheaval. The residential task here includes the paradoxical one of trying to provide some short-term stability and reliability for what is often a rapid turnover of children whose lives have been (temporarily at least) disrupted and unsettled. Staff will require appropriate training, support and leadership if they are to achieve the sort of sensitive and engaged caring that the children will need.

Level two: residential treatment homes

There should also be a number of residential homes whose task is more than providing good 'stabilising' substitute care. The task of these homes will be to provide and harness specialised support and care for children who will largely be from category two: that is, children who have a longer history of difficulty and/or who have complex needs, and who may require a longer period in residential care.

These homes will provide perhaps six to eight beds, and will have a higher staffing ratio than the level one homes. The staff should be trained in the methods of residential treatment, that is, high-quality group work and 'everyday life' work to enable the children to recognise, express and hopefully resolve their unhappiness or distress rather than enacting it through violence or other disturbed behaviour, and to support the children's reconciliation and re-engagement with their families. The homes will need access to a range of specialised support services such as psychiatric and psychological advice, special educational support, employment, counselling or other therapeutic input for individual children, and high levels of supervision and consultancy for the residential staff. The work of the units will need to be planned in conjunction with family support and other services for the children's families, in order to facilitate a return home where this is feasible, for example where change can also be effected within the family. In other cases these children may move on to foster or other substitute care, sometimes on a long-term basis.

Level three: high support units

There should be a small number of residential units located regionally that can offer the most specialised residential care and treatment to young people in category three. These units will provide intensive support and treatment, either on a therapeutic community model for those children assessed as being able to benefit from such an approach, or on a more behaviourally based model, but in each case oriented towards positive change in the child's circumstances, connected where possible to similar changes in the family. Again there will be a need for the appropriate levels and types of staff training and support if these units are to succeed in what will be a most challenging task.

These units should be planned and commissioned by consortia of local authorities on the basis of national policy and perceived regional need, rather than being left either to chance or to the market as perceived by independent providers. They will be equivalent to the 'high support units' developed in the Irish Republic since 1999 (Social Information Systems 2003). The numbers of such units required will clearly depend upon other policy decisions, for example, whether there is a decision to keep more young people out of the juvenile justice or psychiatric inpatient systems.

Management and support of the residential care system

Although the different types of unit that have been outlined above all have different tasks, in terms of their practice and management they are all on the same continuum. They will all need skilled leadership and management, and will require investment in staff with the appropriate skills for each level of task. There will therefore need to be a nationally agreed structure for their management and supervision, and care standards will need to be established for each level of home. The pattern and distribution of each type of home in the Welsh local authorities should be determined nationally and regionally, although the supervision and management of the homes should be at a local level, with consortia delegating management responsibility for the level two and three units.

It is also critical that each home, at whatever level, is led by an expert residential manager who can provide the vision, commitment and leadership qualities to ensure the establishment of a positive caring culture in the home. These managers themselves will need to be supported through line management as well as having access to expert advice and consultancy on child care and staffing issues. The ongoing training and support of these managers, and the establishment across the country of a culture of positive residential care, would be among the tasks of the proposed Welsh centre, models of which are set out below.

Investing in residential staff and managers

The best quality of residential care for children can only be achieved through the development of positive caring cultures in the homes, which will depend primarily on the staff. Any plan to improve residential child care in Wales can only succeed, therefore, if there is a strategy for investing in the professional staff who will run the homes and care for the young people.

We therefore propose that the Welsh Assembly Government should consider establishing a Welsh centre either for residential child care or for child care, which would coordinate and support the necessary positive care culture throughout the residential homes in Wales. Such a centre would take a distinctive Welsh approach to the issues, although it might also draw upon the example of the Scottish Institute for Residential Child Care, which is based at the University of Strathclyde and funded by the Scottish Executive. In England a National Centre for Excellence in Residential Child Care was established in November 2005 by the Department for Education and Skills and located at the National Children's Bureau. The Welsh centre would provide a focus and powerhouse for a renewed investment in residential child care in Wales. It would achieve this through strategies of staff training, support and consultancy for staff at all levels including local authority managers of residential services, as well as through a programme of research and the production of evidence-based guidance for staff. We start with considering a centre focused on residential child care.

Model A: a centre for residential child care

One of the aims of such a centre would be to raise the profile of positive residential child care, and to make it a more attractive career option for young people, including graduates. The hope would be that people would stay longer working in residential care, and might seek promotion within or between the different types of unit. Such career development would need to be supported by programmes of professional training, which in the short term may need to be modified forms of the new social work degree, but which in the long term might evolve into a more specialised and focused child care training, along the lines of either the social pedagogy models in Europe or the child and youth care model in North America and elsewhere.

Another aim of the centre would therefore be to explore and develop new forms of both qualifying and post-qualifying training for residential staff. The task of residential leadership is a particularly demanding one, and there is little post-qualifying or advanced training of any sort currently available for residential child care staff. In England there is the MA in therapeutic child care (due to close in 2006) at Reading University, and in Scotland the MSc in residential care at Strathclyde. If the WAG is to promote and develop high-quality residential services in Wales it should support the establishment of a Welsh post-qualifying/ advanced course in residential care (including management and leadership).

Model B: an interdisciplinary centre for child and youth care in Wales

Another approach, and the one we prefer, is to see the focus of the centre as child care, which differs from both the Scottish and the new English models. The whole field of child care is currently being re-mapped, with the advent of multidisciplinary services such as SureStart and youth offending teams. Each of these new configurations has invested in its own programme of staff training and development, usually in isolation from other disciplines, but sometimes in collaboration with universities and other training providers. These training programmes have been necessary in the short term as new services have established themselves, but the medium-term implication is that, although each of these services may be serving broadly the same population at different stages of childhood, contradictions and disjunctures may begin to arise between the methods, assumptions, theoretical models and codes of practice of the different sectors.

In the medium term, therefore, there may be a case for a coordinated national strategy for the support and care of children and young people in Wales, again given focus and an identifiable base in a centre. This alternative model for a centre would focus not only on residential child care but also on all the other models and settings through which care, support and treatment is provided for young people. Such an approach would require much more coordination between those different fields, but it might thus have more long-term significance for the development of children's services.

Such a broad-based approach would have immense significance for career structures in the field of child care. People would be seen as 'child care specialists' in direct care and would be able to move between settings. Their core skill would be that of working with children and they would need specialist training for different areas of work. This might allow connections to be established at an international level, in particular with other countries in which there is a recognised discipline of professional work with children and young people, such as those described earlier. One of the findings of this research team has been the professional isolation of residential child care services, both within the range of child care services in the UK and internationally in terms of the contrast with the greater professionalisation of child and youth care workers in other developed countries. An interdisciplinary centre for the care of children and young people might help to address this professionalisation in the longer term.

ISSUES REQUIRING FURTHER EXPLORATION

Creating the best environments for residential homes

We have stressed that a lot is known about the key components of good practice such as clear leadership, good relationships between children and staff, coherence between aims and values in the home, management, organisation and welfare system. However, we have noted that much less is known about how to create the conditions in which these factors can be created. This is precisely the sort of topic that could be developed by the Welsh centre, which would be in a position to look at the theoretical underpinning, at the practice implications and then at the processes by which the appropriate work conditions are created and supported. The centre would be able to develop exemplar practice projects.

Evaluating very small homes

The growth in the numbers of homes with one or two residents appears to have developed as providers have sought to find ways to look after children with very disturbed behaviour. We are not aware of any planning that proposed such homes as a good model of provision. We are not in a position to comment on the quality of the provision provided, or on the outcomes for children, as these were not part of our brief. Their usage shows that they fill a need for some local authorities. Since we know of no research studies of homes like these, we suggest that the WAG should commission research of such establishments to examine:

- the characteristics of this style of daily living and the implications for children and staff of living in comparative isolation
- the needs such homes are thought to fulfil
- outcomes
- the costs of provision
- the extent to which regulatory requirements fit such homes.

Meeting the needs of children placed a long distance from home

There is a proper debate to be had as to the advantages and disadvantages of placing a child close to home or in a specialist establishment at a greater distance. In addition it is apparent that there are numbers of children placed in Wales from England and vice versa, as well as children from South Wales placed in the North. There are suggestions that too often there is very poor field social work oversight of the placements that is being reported neither to SSI in England nor to SSIW. Some children face significant cultural isolation, with Welsh-language children being placed in English-speaking areas. In addition, there is hearsay evidence that an increasing number of English and Scottish children placed in North Wales are unable to mix in the local community because the young people are Welsh speaking.

Achieving effective partnership and corporate parenting

Official reports recognise that children's needs cannot be met by any one agency. Yet it is apparent from reports from audit, SSIW and Estyn that whilst there may be some improvement in levels of cooperation, far too often the worthy aspirations of agencies to work together in the interests of the child are not achieved. For example, as we have pointed out in the earlier research review, constructive working relationships between individual staff from a school and a residential home may be of no avail alongside a school or local authority approach that results in excluding large numbers of looked after children while failing to provide any reasonable level of alternative education. Our point is that there are competing pressures and WAG will need to recognise this and demand that local authorities look at the coherence of their own policies. Questions need to be asked simultaneously of those responsible for the local delivery of health, education and social services as to the ways in which they are fulfilling their responsibilities for children.

Agencies under financial pressure are likely to choose the most appropriate and cheapest option *to their agency*. There is no gain for them in choosing services that may be cheaper to the public purse overall but are more costly to their own agency either in the short or long term. The WAG could consider procedures for allocating money to accompany services for a particular child, and then allowing the money to be spent as determined by local planning committees by any of several agencies.

Another means that has been used in health and social care for older people has been to appoint generic workers, able to work in either sector. The WAG could consider whether there are roles for such crossing of boundaries, perhaps for a generic education and child care support worker or, with learning disabled children, health and child care support workers. Some agencies are already providing staff who will liaise with families as they are not willing to rely on the often poor support from local authority field social workers. Again, there could be consideration of whether such staff could form part of a support team for residential homes when under pressure and liaise with families.

Youth justice provides another area where services may be distinct (and possibly divisive) but could be cooperative. Youth justice policies affect the numbers of young people in residential care. However, the ways in which residential staff manage offending behaviour that takes place within their establishments will also impact on the service. Staff have to think about how to control the children and young people in their homes and, whether under pressure from neighbours, managers or in fear of losing control, they involve police too often in minor misbehaviour criminal damage or as a threat to the children. As with any behaviour there should be an attempt to understand and assess: What has happened? What are the reasons? What are the risks? What should be done? In working out how to manage and work with young people whose behaviour is criminal, or borders on criminality, residential staff might well learn skills from staff from youth offending teams. Indeed, staff from youth offending teams could work for short spells in residential homes.

The brief for this study precluded the detailed examination of the quality, level and organisation of fieldwork support for children and young people entering the looked after system. We think, however, that *some* of the problems arising from the placement of young people in both foster and residential care arise from the gaps and failings in fieldwork with children and young people: in the assessment of young people, the ability to communicate effectively with the most troubled young people, and the determination to sustain appropriate levels of contact with young people in substitute care. Some of these difficulties may be due to lack of resources (for example, problems in recruiting, or inadequate staffing levels), and there is a particular problem in the high turnover of field social work staff in some areas but it must be recognised that some of them may also be caused by problems in the skill base or value bases of individuals, teams or their managers. Thus we argue that it will not be possible to make significant improvements in the quality of young people's experience in the care system unless serious attention is paid to the quality of field social work and its management and administration.

Services for children with greater degrees of disturbance

These are the sorts of children who might come under mental health or youth justice systems. Currently they are likely, in a haphazard way dependent on local knowledge of services, local beliefs, and local funding, to go to a highly specialist residential home. Examples of such establishments are a therapeutic community, an adolescent mental health unit, a one bed residential home, a secure unit or youth justice places. We suggest the strategy should, as with all other parts, follow on a proper assessment of need, not just an assessment of behaviour and competence in areas such as education. It is not satisfactory that what happens to such children is haphazard in the way that we describe. The WAG should aim to provide all such young people with the best specialist resources.

We have noted above that moving money between different systems and departments is complex. Thus, it may be cheaper overall to support a young person in a specialist therapeutic community than in a youth justice secure unit. However, the costs to a local authority will be far higher to fund the place in the therapeutic community if other agencies have to contribute to funding a placement in the youth justice system. Developing imaginative systems where the money can follow the young person would make an immense difference to the development of the best resources. Further, the difficulty of working with the most disturbed young people should be recognised. It seems clear that many local authorities have chosen to avoid the problems of working with highly disturbed young people, and prefer to see them managed by private providers or within health or youth justice systems. Such an approach may be understandable and, within Wales, may have been influenced by the recognition of the highly damaging residential care on which the Waterhouse report commented. However, this does not seem satisfactory within the context of a child care service committed to meeting children's needs in a planned and responsive way. We suggest that the WAG consider systems to reward both in recognition and resources those authorities that are willing to consider ways to make the best resources available to young people who come within this category.

The discussion above considers how to meet the needs of young people who might be placed in the youth justice or local authority systems. There are parallels with the complexity of how to provide properly for young people with significant psychiatric problems. It has been stressed to us that psychiatrists see their task as working with people with what they perceive as identifiable mental health conditions. In practice, this means that they will probably choose not to work with young people in the looked after system, many of whose difficulties are conduct disorders and thus not readily within the scope of psychiatric treatment. More careful diagnosis might lead to greater recognition in practice of the depth of distress and depression reflected in the research reports discussed earlier. A model for the development of such an approach in Scotland has been outlined by Milligan (2002). This discussion again highlights the need for child care social workers to develop a more sophisticated and standardised approach to the assessment of emotional and psychological need, if they are to enable young people to access the appropriate type and level of specialist support.

The dilemmas as to which agency should provide a service are compounded in this area by the shortage of child psychiatrists. We have noted the high numbers of young people in the 'looked after' system with moderate and severe levels of emotional and behavioural difficulty. It is imperative that young people and staff can access support and that there is clarity about responsibility for service provision. The complexity of the work is compounded by the lack of a shared language between mental health and social services staff, and the lack of much work undertaken on a multidisciplinary basis. It should be noted that in some parts of the UK there are closer ties between community mental health teams (CMHTs) and residential services, in the form of support for individual young people and for staff. Such connections should be explored. In addition, there are some conditions such as conduct disorders or speech deficiencies that do not fit administrative categories.

The quality of daily living and the measuring of performance by targets

Amidst the structural factors that make the activity of residential care difficult and that limit the life chances of children when they leave establishments, it is easy to despair of doing anything worthwhile. However, it is essential for residential staff and their managers to recognise that the quality of daily life does matter and that whatever pressures there are, much of what happens in daily living is within the control of the home and the organisation responsible for it.

The WAG should review the outcomes set for residential care and the targets that are used to assess their performance. The outcomes and the targets should reflect the reality of the task and the fundamental objectives or primary task. Our concern is that there may be occasions when endeavouring to meet the target may lead people away from what ought to be their core focus. For example, in terms of education it is more important to assess the start and finish points of an individual child's stay in the looked after system, than the numbers achieving set grades in certain subjects at GCSE. We have heard of teachers of looked after children who think that they cannot focus on the educational needs of a child as they assess the child, because they are required to press for performance in maths and English.

There is a temptation for politicians and policy-makers to think that legislation and guidance will transform a service. Yet a study of the quality of practice may show this not to be the case. Thus, the Children Act (1989) and Volume 4 of the guidance addressed many of the key requirements on residential staff very clearly; while the subsequent standards have spelled out what good quality residential child care should look like. The government's assessment framework outlines the chief components in the planning of children's care. This is an approach that has been successful in legislating for better practice, and it was indeed very necessary in the wake of the revelations of abuse, neglect and oppression in children's residential services in all parts of the UK during the latter part of the 20th century.

There is nevertheless a limit to which legislation on its own, however much it is embellished and supported by official guidance and recommendation, can in itself improve the quality of practice. Legislation can only operate at a pragmatic level, emphasising factors such as 'minimum requirements', basic competencies or human rights; it cannot easily deal with pain, confusion and distress. In the same way as ignoring the structural factors in the lives of children and families is both naïve and ineffective, similarly the structures, systems and processes in which residential homes operate have a critical impact on what happens in residential homes.

CONCLUSION: A RESIDENTIAL CHILD CARE STRATEGY FOR WALES

We conclude by setting out some significant planning and structural factors that will impact on the quality of fostering and residential services in Wales.

■ There must be an audit of the numbers of children in different parts of the system. This should be used for planning purposes to show what is the current position and thus to lead to consideration of the resources needed by local authorities.

- The Welsh Assembly Government and local authorities must be in a position to drive forward their policies. Thus, whether local authorities provide services directly themselves or commission them from others, they should have access to the resources that they need. They should not be content with using the services that happen to be provided by others: such services may not meet the needs of children and may be a second best alternative, used because the best provision does not exist.
- Local authorities should be in a position to differentiate between children, considering their needs and planning appropriately. Assessment is the key to this. However, the act of conducting an assessment, however good the assessment framework, does not ensure that their assessment material is used to look at the services that are appropriate for that child. Too frequently, rather than looking at the needs of a child, staff will try various options in sequence, starting with less specialist foster care; if this fails, then a series of moves are likely through different types of foster care before different types of residential care are tried. We argue that assessment should be used to plan for a child, which might lead to some children being placed, appropriately, earlier in a residential home.
- There are serious questions about the use that is made of records. Information collected should be accumulated to provide details of the ways that resources are used. There is no point in demanding time consuming records if they are not used for review and planning.
- There is a strong case for the establishment of a Welsh centre, which would spearhead the collection and use of information on children. Tasks for such a centre could include proposing topics for research and developing good practice guidance from research evidence. It should also have the function of a staff development college, leading the debate as to how staff working in child care are best trained.

References and further reading

Abbott, D, Morris, J and Ward, L (2000) *Disabled Children and Residential Schools: A survey of local authority policy and practice.* Bristol: Norah Fry Research Centre.

Ainsworth, F (1997) *Family Centred Group Care: Model building.* Aldershot: Ashgate.

Anglin, J (2002) *Pain, Normality and the Struggle for Congruence: Reinterpreting residential care for children and youth.* Binghamton, NY: Haworth Press.

Axford, N (2003) *Child Well-being from Different Perspectives: Measuring and responding to unmet need, violated rights, poverty, poor quality of life and social exclusion.* Dartington Social Research Unit.

Balbernie, R (1966) *Residential Work with Children.* London: Pergamon.

Baldwin, N (1990) *The Power to Care in Children's Homes: Experiences of residential workers.* Aldershot: Avebury.

Barter, C, Renold, E, Berridge, D and Cawson, P (2004) *Peer Violence in Children's Residential Care.* Basingstoke: Palgrave Macmillan.

Beedell, C (1970) *Residential Life with Children.* London: Routledge and Kegan Paul.

Beedell, C and Clough, R (1992) Evidence submitted to Department of Health (1992) *Choosing with Care. The report of the Committee of Inquiry into the selection, development and management of staff in children's homes.* London: HMSO.

Beresford, B 'Preventing the social exclusion of disabled children' in McNeish, D, Newman, T and Roberts, H (2002) *What Works for Children?* Buckingham: Open University Press.

Berridge, D (1985) *Children's Homes.* Oxford: Blackwell.

Berridge, D 'Residential care' in McNeish, D, Newman, T and Roberts, H (2002) *What Works for Children?* Buckingham: Open University Press.

Berridge, D and Brodie, I (1998) *Children's Homes Revisited.* London: Jessica Kingsley.

Berry, J (1975) *Daily Experience in Residential Life: A study of children and their care-givers.* London: Routledge and Kegan Paul.

Bettelheim, B (1950) *Love is Not Enough.* New York: Free Press.

Biehal, N, Clayden, M, Stein, M and Wade, J (1995) *Moving On: Young people and leaving care schemes.* London: HMSO.

Boston, M and Szur, R (1983) *Psychotherapy with Severely Deprived Children.* London: Karnac Books.

Broad, B (1998) *Young People Leaving Care.* London: Jessica Kingsley.

Brown, A and Clough, R (1989) *Groups and Groupings. Life and work in day and residential settings.* London: Tavistock.

Brown, E, Bullock, R, Hobson, C and Little, M (1998) *Making Residential Care Work: Structure and culture in children's homes.* Aldershot: Ashgate.

Bullock, R, Little, M, and Millham, S (1993) *Residential Care for Children: A review of the research.* London: HMSO.

Bullock, R, Little, M and Millham, S (1998) *Secure Treatment Outcomes: The care careers of very difficult adolescents.* Aldershot: Ashgate.

Burton, J (1993) *The Handbook of Residential Care.* London: Routledge.

Burton, J (1998) *Managing Residential Care.* London: Routledge.

Cairns, K (2002) *Attachment, Trauma and Resilience: Therapeutic caring for children.* London: BAAF.

Carter, J 'The meaning of good experience' in Ward, A, Kasinski, K, Pooley, J, and Worthington, A (eds) (2003) *Therapeutic Communities for Children and Young People.* London: Jessica Kingsley.

Cawson, P, Berridge, D, Barter, C and Renold, E (2001) *Physical and Sexual Violence Between Children in Residential Settings: Exploring perspectives and experiences*. Research report for the Economic and Social Research Council.

Chakrabarti, M and Hill, M (eds) (2000) *Residential Child Care: International perspectives on links with families and peers*. London: Jessica Kingsley.

Chipenda-Dansokho, S and the Centre for Social Policy (2003) 'The determinants and influence of size on residential settings for children', *International Journal of Child and Family Welfare*, VI, 66–76.

Chipenda-Dansokho, S, Little, M and Thomas, B (2003) *Residential Services for Children: Definitions, numbers and classifications*. Chicago: Chapin Hall Center for Children, University of Chicago.

Clough, R (2000) *The Practice of Residential Work*. Basingstoke: Macmillan.

Clough, R and McCoy, K (2000) *An Audit of the Working Practices of the Social Services Inspectorate, Wales*. Report presented to the National Assembly for Wales. Cardiff: SSIW.

Cooper, A (2005) *The Children's Workforce in England: A review of the evidence*. London: DfES.

Crimmens, D and Pitts, J (2000) *Positive Residential Practice: Learning the lessons of the 1990s*. Lyme Regis: Russell House Publishing.

Dartington Social Research Unit (2002) *Practice Tools: Matching needs and services; Paperwork: The clinical assessment of children in need; Aggregated Data: Better management information and planning in children's services; Prediction: Perspectives on diagnosis, prognosis and interventions for children in need*.

Davey, D (2002) *Key Factors that Influence the Educational Experience and Achievement of Children Looked After: A case study of young people placed in residential and foster care in South Wales*. Cardiff: Cardiff University.

Davison, A (1995) *Residential Care: The provision of quality care in residential and educational group care settings*. Aldershot: Arena.

Department of Health (DH) (1991) *Children in the Public Care*. London: HMSO.

Department of Health (1998) *Caring for Children Away from Home: Messages from research*. Chichester: John Wiley and Sons.

Department of Health (2001) *Outcome Indicators for Looked After Children: Year Ending 30 September 2000*. London: Department of Health.

Department of Health (2002) *National Statistics, Children Looked After by Local Authorities, Year Ending 31 March 2001, England*. London: The Stationery Office.

Department of Health (2003a) *The Integrated Children's System Conceptual Framework*. London: Department of Health.

Department of Health (2003b) *Choice Protects Update Bulletin No 2, March 2003*. London: Department of Health.

DfES (2003) *Green Paper: Every Child Matters*. London: Stationery Office.

Dimigen, G, Del Priore, C, Butler, S, Evans, S, Ferguson, L and Swan, M (1999) 'Psychiatric disorder among children at time of entering local authority care: questionnaire survey', *British Medical Journal*, 319 (7211), 675.

Dockar-Drysdale, B (1990) *The Provision of Primary Experience: Winnicottian work with children and adolescents*. London: Free Association.

Douglas, T (1986) *Group Living: The application of group dynamics in residential settings*. London: Tavistock.

Emond, R (2002) 'Understanding the resident group', *Scottish Journal of Residential Child Care*, 1 (1), 30–40.

Emond, R 'An outsider's view of the inside' in Crimmens, D and Milligan, I (eds) (2005) *Facing Forward. Residential child care in the 21st century*. Lyme Regis: Russel House.

Fahlberg, V (ed) (1990) *Residential Treatment: A tapestry of many therapies*. Indianapolis: Perspectives Press.

Frost, N, Mills, S and Stein, M (1999) *Understanding Residential Child Care*. Aldershot: Ashgate.

Goffman, E (1961) *Asylums*. New York: Doubleday.

Gooch, D (1996) 'Home and away: the residential care, education and control of children in historical and political context', *Child and Family Social Work*, I, 19–32.

Hagell, A, Hazel, N and Shaw, C (2000) *Evaluation of Medway Secure Training Centre*. London: Policy Research Bureau.

Hicks, L, Gibbs, I, Byford, S and Weatherley, H (2003) *Leadership and Resources in Children's Homes*. University of York: Social Work Research and Development Unit.

Hill, M 'Inclusiveness in residential care' in Chakrabarti, M and Hill, M (eds) (2000) *Residential Child Care: International perspectives on links with families and peers*. London: Jessica Kingsley.

Hills, D and Child, C (1998) *Leadership in Residential Child Care. Evaluating qualification training*. Chichester: Wiley.

Home Office (1914) *Report of the Chief Inspector*, Cd. 8091. London: Home Office.

Howe, D (1995) *Attachment Theory for Social Work Practice*. Basingstoke: Macmillan.

Hunter, M (2001) *Psychotherapy with Young People in Care: Lost and found*. Hove: Brunner-Routledge.

Kahan, B (1979) *Growing Up in Care*. Oxford: Blackwell.

Kahan, B (1995) *Growing Up in Groups*. London: HMSO.

King, R, Raynes, N and Tizard, J (1973) *Patterns of Residential Care*. London: Routledge and Kegan Paul.

Lambert, R and Millham, S (1968) *The Hothouse Society: An exploration of boarding school life through boys' and girls' own writings*. London: Weidenfeld and Nicolson.

Lambert, R, Millham, S and Bullock, R (1975) *The Chance of a Lifetime? A survey of boys' and co-educational boarding schools in England and Wales*. London: Weidenfeld and Nicolson.

Learndirect (2006) Social worker: residential: training http://www.learndirect-advice.co.uk/helpwithyourcareer/jobprofiles/profiles/profile633/

Little, M (1990) *Young Men in Prison: The criminal identity explored through the rules of behaviour*. Aldershot: Dartmouth.

Little, M and Kelly, S (1995) *A Life without Problems? The achievements of a therapeutic community*. Aldershot: Arena.

Little, M, Kogan, J, Bullock, R and van der Laan, P (2004) 'ISSP: An experiment in multisystemic responses to persistent young offenders known to children's services', *British Journal of Criminology*, 44, 225–40.

Little, M, Kohm, A and Thompson, R (2005) 'The impact of residential placement on child development: research and policy implications', *International Journal of Social Welfare*, XIV, 200–9.

Mainey, A (2004) *Better Than You Think: staff morale, qualifications and retention in residential childcare*. London: National Children's Bureau.

McCann, J, James, A, Wilson, S and Dunn, G (1996) 'Prevalence of psychiatric disorders of young people in the care system', *British Medical Journal*, 313, 1529–30.

McNeish, D, Newman, T and Roberts, H (2002) *What Works for Children?* Buckingham: Open University Press.

Meltzer, H, Corbin, T, Gatward, R, Goodman, R and Ford, T (2002) *The Mental Health of Young People Looked After by Local Authorities in England.* Summary Report. A survey carried out by the Social Survey Division of ONS on behalf of the Department of Health. HMSO London.

Menzies Lyth, E 'Introduction' in Davies, R (ed) (1997) *Stress in Social Work*. London: Jessica Kingsley.

Miller, E and Gwynne, G (1972) *A Life Apart: A pilot study of residential institutions for the physically handicapped and the young chronic sick*. London: Tavistock.

Millham, S, Bullock, R and Cherrett, P (1975) *After Grace – Teeth: A comparative study of the residential experience of boys in approved schools.* London: Chaucer Press.

Millham, S, Bullock, R, Hosie, K and Haak, M (1986) *Lost in Care: The problems of maintaining links between children in care and their families.* Aldershot: Gower.

Milligan, I (2002) *Innovations in Mental Health Services: Meeting the mental health needs of 'looked after' young people in Scotland*. Paper delivered at 7th EUSARF Congress, Trondheim, Norway.

Morpeth, L (2004) *Organisation and Outcomes in Children's Services*, PhD thesis, University of Exeter.

Morris, J (1998) *Still Missing? The experiences of disabled children and young people living away from their families*, Volume 1, London: Who Cares? Trust.

Morris, J (2000) *Having Someone Who Cares: Barriers to change in the public care of children*. London: National Children's Bureau.

Moss, P 'Residential care of children: a general view' in Tizard, J, Sinclair, I and Clarke, R (eds) (1975) *Varieties of Residential Experience*. London: Routledge and Kegan Paul.

National Assembly for Wales (1999a) *New Arrangements for Young People Living in and Leaving Care* (July). Cardiff: National Assembly for Wales.

National Assembly for Wales (1999b) *Adoption: Achieving the right balance* (December). Cardiff: National Assembly for Wales.

National Assembly for Wales (2000a) *Framework for the Assessment of Children in Need and Their Families*. Cardiff: National Assembly for Wales.

National Assembly for Wales (2000b) *Looking After Children: Assessing outcomes in child care – strategy for revisions* (February). Cardiff: National Assembly for Wales.

National Assembly for Wales (2000c) *Practice Guide to Investigate Allegations of Abuse Against a Professional or Carer in Relation to Children Looked After*. Cardiff: National Assembly for Wales.

National Assembly for Wales (2000d) *Promoting Health for Looked After Children: A guide to healthcare planning, assessment and monitoring*. Cardiff: National Assembly for Wales.

National Assembly for Wales (2000e) *Response to Lost in Care*. Cardiff: National Assembly for Wales.

National Assembly for Wales (2000f) *Social Services White Paper for Wales, 'Building for the Future' Implementation Plan*. Cardiff: National Assembly for Wales.

National Assembly for Wales (2000g) *Working Together to Safeguard Children*. Cardiff: National Assembly for Wales.

National Assembly for Wales (2001a) *Child and Adolescent Mental Health Services – Everybody's Business – Strategy Document*. Cardiff: National Assembly for Wales.

National Assembly for Wales (2001b) *Guidance on the Education of Children Looked After by Local Authorities, Circular 2/2001*. Cardiff: National Assembly for Wales.

National Assembly for Wales (2002) *Too Serious a Thing: The review of safeguards for children and young people treated and cared for by the NHS in Wales*. Cardiff: National Assembly for Wales.

National Assembly for Wales (2003) *Consultation Paper: Improving placement choice and stability for children and young people looked after – strategic framework*. Cardiff: National Assembly for Wales.

Page, R (1978) *Who Cares?* London: National Children's Bureau.

Parker, R (1966) *Decisions in Child Care*. London: Allen and Unwin.

Parker, R 'Children' in Sinclair, I (1988) *Residential Care: The research reviewed*. London: HMSO.

Pitts, J 'The dismal state of the secure estate' in Crimmens, D and Milligan, I (2005) *Facing Forward: Residential child care in the 21st century*. Lyme Regis, Russell House Publishing, pp. 186–97.

Pooley, J 'Keeping families in mind' in Ward, A, Kasinski, K, Pooley, J, and Worthington, A (eds) (2003) *Therapeutic Communities for Children and Young People*. London: Jessica Kingsley.

Residential Forum (1998) *A Golden Opportunity*. London: Residential Forum.

Rose, J (2002) *Working with Young People in Secure Accommodation*. Hove: Brunner-Routledge.

Rose, M (1990) *Healing Hurt Minds: The Peper Harow experience*. London: Tavistock/Routledge.

Rose, M (1997) *Transforming Hate to Love*. London, Routledge.

Rushton, A 'Residential and foster care' in Rutter, M and Taylor, E (eds) (2002) *Child and Adolescent Psychiatry*, 4th edition. Oxford: Blackwell.

Rutter, M (2000) 'Children in substitute care: some conceptual considerations and research implications', *Children and Youth Services Review*, 22, 9/10, 685–703.

Scottish Institute for Residential Child Care (SIRCC) www.sircc.strath.ac.uk/

Secretary of State for Health (1998) *The Government's Response to the Children's Safeguards Review*, CM4105. London: HMSO.

Shaw, C (1998) *Remember My Messages: The experiences and views of 2,000 children in public care in the UK*. London: Who Cares? Trust.

Sinclair, I and Gibbs, I (1998) *Children's Homes: A study in diversity*. Chichester: John Wiley and Sons.

Sinclair, R, Garnett, L and Berridge, D (1995) *Social Work and Assessment with Adolescents*. London: National Children's Bureau.

Social Information Systems (2003) *Definition and Usage of High Support in Ireland*. Report to the Special Residential Services Board. Dublin: Special Residential Services Board.

Social Services Data Activity. *SSDA 903*. Local Government Data Unit, Wales.

Social Services Inspectorate (SSI) (1993) *Corporate Parents. Inspection of residential child care services in 11 local authorities*, November 1992–March 1993. London: Department of Health.

Social Services Inspectorate for Wales (SSIW) (2001) *Educational Provision for Looked After Children*. Cardiff: SSIW.

Social Services Inspectorate for Wales (SSIW) (2003) Unpublished reports from discussions with Disability Network.

Stanley, D and Reed, J (1999) *Opening Up Care. Achieving principled practice in health and social care institutions*. London: Arnold.

Statham, J and Greenfields, M (2005) 'Part-time fostering: recruiting and supporting carers for short break schemes', *Adoption and Fostering*, XXIX, 33–41.

Stein, M and Carey, K (1986) *Leaving Care*. Oxford: Blackwell.

Stevenson, O (1968) 'Reception into care – its meaning for all concerned' in Tod, R (ed) (1968) *Children in Care*. London: Longman.

Support Force for Residential Care (1995) *Good Care Matters*. London: Department of Health.

Tizard, B (1986) *The Care of Young Children: Implications of recent research*. London: University of London Institute of Education.

Tizard, J, Sinclair, I and Clarke, R (eds) (1975) *Varieties of Residential Experience*. London: Routledge and Kegan Paul.

Topss UK (2003) *The National Occupational Standards for Managers in Residential Child Care*. London: Topss UK.

Trieschman, A, Whittaker, J and Brendtro, L (1969) *The Other 23 Hours: Child-care work with emotionally-disturbed children in a therapeutic milieu*. New York: Aldine.

Utting, W (1997) *People Like Us: The report of the review of safeguards for children living away from home.* London: Department of Health.

Wagner, G (1988) *A Positive Choice.* London: HMSO.

Wales Assembly Government (2002) *Children and Young People's Framework: Planning Guidance.* Cardiff: National Assembly for Wales.

Walton, R and Elliott, D (eds) (1980) *Residential Care: A reader in current theory and practice.* Oxford: Pergamon.

Ward, A (1996) 'Opportunity led work part 2: the framework'. *Social Work Education.* 8 (1), 67–78.

Ward, A and McMahon, L (eds) (1998) *Intuition is Not Enough: Matching learning with practice in therapeutic child care.* London: Routledge.

Ward, A (2002) 'Opportunity led work: maximising the possibilities for therapeutic communication in everyday interactions', *Therapeutic Communities*, 23 (2) 111–24.

Ward, A (2006, in press) *Working in Group Care. Social work and social care in residential and day care settings* (2nd edn). Bristol: Policy Press.

Ward, A, Kasinski, K, Pooley, J, and Worthington, A (eds) (2003) *Therapeutic Communities for Children and Young People.* London: Jessica Kingsley.

Waterhouse, R, Clough, M and le Fleming, M (2000) *Lost in Care: Report of the tribunal of inquiry into the abuse of children in care in the former county council areas of Gwynedd and Clwyd since 1974*, HC 21. London: HMSO.

Whipp, R, Kirkpatrick, I and Kitchener, M (2005) *Managing Residential Care: A managed service.* Basingstoke, Palgrave MacMillan.

Whitaker, D, Archer, L and Hicks, L (1998) *Working in Children's Homes: Challenges and complexities.* Chichester: John Wiley and Sons.

Whittaker, J (1979) *Caring for Troubled Children.* San Francisco: Jossey-Bass.

Wolkind, S and Rushton, M 'Residential and foster care' in Rutter, M, Taylor, E and Hersov, L (eds) (1994) *Child and Adolescent Psychiatry: Modern approaches*, 3rd edition. Oxford: Blackwell.

Youth Justice Board (2003) Website: http://www.youth-justice-board.gov.uk/ YouthJusticeBoard/Custody/

Index